LEN HURST
CHAMPION BELTER

The story of Len Hurst, Britain's first Marathon Champion

LEN HURST
CHAMPION BELTER

The story of Len Hurst, Britain's first Marathon Champion

ALEX WILSON

CONTENTS

CONTENTS

PROLOGUE

It was the greatest win in the history of the London to Brighton race. The winner smashed the previous record by over 26 minutes and finished over 40 minutes clear of the opposition. He was dressed and having a drink when the second placed man arrived. The vintage championship belt, awarded to the winning team in the London to Brighton road race from 1951-2005, was one of the last reminders of this great athlete, who held the Brighton record longer than any other did. He was the world's greatest marathon runner of his day.

Sporting Life, the leading British sporting newspaper, hailed him the 'greatest distance runner of the century'.

He would have been an overwhelming gold-medal favourite in the marathon race at the inaugural Olympic Games in 1896, and again at Paris four years hence, except for one minor yet crucial detail: he was a professional.

FOREWORD

Len Hurst was a remarkable athlete. Not only did he perform at the highest level across a range of distances, his career also spanned the period from the 19th century pedestrians to the Marathon Mania that followed Dorando Pietri's disqualification at the 1908 London Olympics.

Len Hurst's career first intrigued me in the 1980s and I was fortunate enough to be in contact with one of his sons. This was to give me insights into the background and family life of a professional runner at the turn of the 20th century when writing the original article.

Alex Wilson has taken my original biographical article and has greatly expanded its detail and background through his researches and language skills. This book now gives a unique insight into the tough life of professional runners over 100 years ago. It reveals the necessary inter-action with opponents, the networking and promotion involved in sustaining that often precarious profession.

Len Hurst was the first great marathon runner, he was a pioneer, competing abroad regularly. This important book not only details his career, it illuminates a previously little-known period of global distance running.

Andy Milroy, 26 July 2019.

INTRODUCTION

When Len Hurst died from liver cirrhosis at the age of 65, his demise caused barely a ripple. That was in 1937.

The country had endured the bloodiest war in its history, and after that a decade of austerity and tentative recovery. Now it was facing the real prospect of another war, and yet more bloodshed and hardship. People could be forgiven for forgetting.

The extraordinary life of Len Hurst is, however, a cracking story well worth recollecting. In 1937, the name Len Hurst was but a distant memory to those who had witnessed him perform at the height of his fame. And yet, he was a sporting superstar who in his prime commanded reams of newsprint; a record-breaker with a reputation for integrity; a real crowd-puller.

In the twilight of Queen Victoria's long reign and for some time after, he was the king of British long-distance running. He was not only the first Briton to run the marathon, but also the first to set a recognised world best in this event. These were, admittedly, the fledgling years of the marathon, when the benchmark distance was 25 miles – not 26 miles 385 yards as we know it today. However, the magnitude and significance of Len Hurst's achievements cannot be understated.

After the inaugural Olympic Games of 1896, marathon races were in vogue in France and the USA, but, alas, not in the modern athletics motherland, Britain, where they were virtually unknown until 1908. How then could, of all people, a Briton contrive to be the world's leading exponent of this event? The answer to this mystery will be revealed.

THE EARLY YEARS

Leonard Hurst was born in Sittingbourne on 28 December, 1871. He was one of six children. His mother, Eliza, was a dealer in old clothes. His father, Edward, was a brickmaker and occasional horse trader – the 19th-century equivalent of a used-car salesman. The Hursts were your typical working-class family. They lived in a red brick tenement on Milton Road, a short distance from the railway station.

The working-class housing of the day was basic, utilitarian, spartan, damp, draughty and typically very cramped.

The Sittingbourne of Len Hurst's youth was a small industrial town with a population of some 8,000. The ubiquitous burning of coal in homes and in factories, and the plumes of grey-black smoke rising from the brickfields, meant the denizens of Sittingbourne were constantly living under a pall of smoke and smog. As if air pollution was not bad enough in itself, working-class men of Victorian times were inveterate smokers. Smoking – much like beer drinking – was a popular pastime in which, yes, even long-distance runners indulged.

Owing to poor living and working conditions, not to mention the scourge of disease, the average life expectancy of a working-class male in 1870 was just 45.

The principal industries in Sittingbourne in 1870 were papermaking and brickmaking, and the men of the Hurst family were all employed at the brickworks. Brickmaking was brutal, physical labour. An average brickmaker would work eight to 10 hours a day during the brickmaking season, which was typically from April to October.

Working on a piecework basis, a brickmaker was paid a fixed rate per 1,000 bricks made. In the 1880s an experienced brickmaker could earn around 30 shillings for a good week's work. It was enough to feed and clothe his family and keep a roof over their heads, but barely enough for the comforts of life, such as a quart of beer at sixpence a bottle.

With a quarter of the population living at or below subsistence level, children were still expected to earn their keep.

It wasn't until 1880 that school became compulsory for children aged between five and ten. When Len left school at the age of 12, he headed straight for the brickfields, rolled up his sleeves and got to work. He would eventually become a moulder, which was the most skilful of the brickmaking occupations. With the cost of living being as it was, however, any supplementary income was, of course, welcome.

When Len came into the world a host of political changes were afoot and much-needed labour reforms were being undertaken by the British government. Before the labour reforms, workers had been labouring all the hours under the sun – 60 to 70 hour working weeks had been the norm. The drudgery of the daily grind meant that working-class people had neither the time nor inclination for leisure pursuits.

Children as young as nine had been expected to do menial labour for up to nine hours a day. The labour reforms had an immensely liberating effect led to a great upsurge in sporting activity throughout the British Isles.

1871, the year of Len's birth, marked the introduction of 'bank holidays', and the first sporting fetes in Sittingbourne.

The foot races were especially popular, and the winners were championed. With the added incentive of prize money, standards improved rapidly. Sittingbourne became a centre of excellence for pedestrianism. The professional foot racing scene in Sittingbourne was spearheaded by a publican named James 'Jem' Bailey.

Bailey first made his mark on the running tracks in 1875. An insatiable appetite for training catapulted him to the forefront of British distance running, and in 1878 he came second in the professional ten-mile championship at Lillie Bridge. The following year he defeated British 10-mile champion George Hazael to win the British 50-mile championship. Bailey also set world records for 25 miles (2:41:36 in 1881) and 30 miles (3:18:17 in 1879).

The feats of Jem Bailey inspired other residents of Sittingbourne to follow in his footsteps. Sportsmen from all quarters congregated at his establishment, the Golden Eagle. One of Bailey's many emulators was Joe Hurst, Len's elder brother. Joe took up running in 1878 and soon made a name for himself as a 'stayer'.

Several other runners, or 'peds' as they were known, from the Sittingbourne hot bed would go on to make a name for themselves in six-day races, which were immensely popular at the time. Aside from

The Golden Eagle as it looked around World War One.

Jem Bailey and Joe Hurst, the most notable of these were George Pettit and Harry Vandepeer. From about 1878 athletic sports meetings were held on a regular basis at Gore Court Park and at Bapchild Park. Both venues were located a mile or so from the brickmaking centre of Sittingbourne where the air was eminently more breathable.

As George Bailey's star began to fade, Joe rose to the top of the Sittingbourne professional running scene.

'Popgun', as he was known to his friends, was a regular prize winner throughout

East Kent in races from one to ten miles. He did his training in his spare time after finishing his day's work at the brickworks, and as one can imagine, this was no easy task.

Joe, however, like all professional runners, was driven by the allure of prize money.

In 1887 he became a minor celebrity when he sensationally defeated George Cartwright, the professional 50-mile world record holder, in a 30-mile running match at Sittingbourne. Taking the lead at 18 miles, Joe forced the pace to such effect that the hapless Cartwright quickly fell back, retiring a mile further on. At the completion of 20 miles, Joe was timed at 2:04:30. This was exceptional running on a grass track.

The match won, Joe ran on for two more laps, and at the finish he reportedly looked as fresh as when he had started. Four years later, Joe would produce a similar performance in a match against time at Lea Bridge, where he covered 19 miles 1,020 yards in two hours for a bet of £60.

As a youngster, Len idolised his elder brother. There was a significant age gap between the two, Joe being 13 years Len's senior, but they were both cut from the same cloth. They shared not only a love of running, but also the same placid temperament and self-discipline so fundamental to a career in professional sport. Joe saw in his younger brother the same natural talent and steely resolve; a natural gift to be nurtured.

Two other members of the Hurst family – Harry and Teddy – were also professional runners, albeit of the more casual sort; neither enjoyed, nor aspired to, the same success as Len and Joe.

When he turned 15, Len was welcomed into the fold under the tutelage of his brother and Jem Bailey.

Len at this time ran flat-footed, so they christened him 'The Plodder'. With practice, however, he learned to run more on his forefoot. It was not quite the case of an ugly duckling turning into a graceful swan, but the improvement in running style was transformative in performance terms.

When Len Hurst entered the fray the long-distance running and walking craze, which had begun in the late 1870s, had pretty much run its course. During the 1880s British distance-running stars like George Hazael, Charley Rowell and George Littlewood had raised the bar so high, their records would last until well into the 20th century. In fact, Littlewood's six-day walking record of 531 miles 800 yards, set in 1882, still stands to this day.

Moreover, the sport of professional foot racing was losing its popular grip, with the advent of cycle racing following the invention of the safety bicycle in the mid-1880s. By the late 1880s more and more venues that had once vibrated to the hypnotic thump of runners' feet were now echoing to the click and whirr of chain-driven bicycles.

Another factor depriving professional sport of its lifeblood was the rise in the popularity of amateur athletics and, specifically, the mushrooming of harrier clubs, which were attracting a new breed of working-class amateur. Nevertheless, the idea of running for money still appealed to many, and pedestrianism continued to thrive in small pockets of the country, particularly in the Midlands, Wales, the South East and Scotland. A clutch of enterprising sports promoters and syndicates had succeeded in turning sprint handicaps into profitable commercial ventures. The sprint handicaps, at venues such as the Powderhall Grounds in Edinburgh, the Hyde Park Grounds in Sheffield and the Old Bow Running Grounds in East London, attracted hundreds of entries and were hotly contested. These very same venues also hosted miscellaneous other sports and pastimes such as dog racing, cycle racing, etc.

It was this diversity that made such venues economically viable.

Distance running races were less popular in participation terms and, therefore, tended to be less of a money spinner than, say, sprints, but they were always a popular attraction with spectators and bookmakers alike, and were often framed as the main event at meetings, especially if noted athletes such as Len Hurst were competing.

Len made his professional racing debut at the age of 16 and immediately showed a real aptitude for the long distances. His first race was in his home town over four miles and he won the second prize of £1 10s. Later that year he finished a promising fifth in a ten-mile race.

In his first season, he, or so he would later claim, won 31 races at distances from four to ten miles. His staying power belied his youthful age. In 1889 he contested both the four and ten-mile events at the Sittingbourne Whit Monday sports. After front running his way to the £3 first prize in the four-mile handicap off 880 yards, he took fifth in the ten-mile event.

'Hurst,' wrote the *East Kent Gazette*, commenting on his win in the four-mile race, 'who is a lad of about 17 years of age, maintained his lead well and won easily.'

After making such a promising start to his career, Len was conspicuous by his absence from competition between 1889 and 1891. When Andy Milroy interviewed his son, the late Alf Hurst, in around 1990 for an article in the Road Runners Club Newsletter, he learned that the young professional's career had been stalled by illness, and that he had lost a lot of weight as a result. Although Alf Hurst could not say exactly what his father had been ill with, an outbreak of typhoid fever did in fact occur in Sittingbourne in around 1889 or 1890. It is supposed to have originated through the drinking by some brickfield labourers of water from a shallow well which was contaminated with sewage.

Eventually, encouraged by Joe, Len recovered and went back into training, although it took him some time to regain his old form.

In around 1891 Joe, together with his wife, Emma, and their three children, Ada, Leonard and Lilly, moved to Tottenham and took Len with them. The move is likely to have been prompted by Joe's desire to be closer to East London's thriving professional foot racing scene.

They lived just a stone's throw from meccas of pedestrianism such as the White Hart Grounds at Tottenham Hale, the Old Bow Running Grounds in Glaucus Street, the Excelsior Baths in Bethnal Green, Brown's Grounds in Nunhead, the Old Clay Hall Athletic Grounds in Old Ford Road and the Invicta Grounds in Plumstead, not to mention the running tracks at Enfield, Poplar, Canning Town and Barking, among others.

To keep themselves, they began work in the Edmonton Brickfields. Len was a steady, hardworking and conscientious man and soon became head of a team of men capable of producing 8,000 bricks in 12 hours.

On Monday, 6 June 1892, there was a large crowd assembled at Brown's Grounds in Nunhead to witness the pedestrian and bicycle fete promoted by J.T. Hulls. The main event was a one-hour go-as-you-please handicap featuring Len on scratch and 50-year-old Tom Kirby, of Kentish Town, off 270 yards.

Len reportedly ran in fine style, taking the lead in the last few minutes and, with a distance of 10 miles 40 yards, secured the first prize of a timepiece. In addition to winning the race, he had also, finally, won his long battle against illness.

On 1 October Len entered another one-hour handicap at the Old Bow Running Grounds in the east end of London.

Wretched weather kept the attendance down and made for heavy going, and despite his earlier success at Nunhead, Len received a start of 3 ½ laps, or 948 yards, the track being 6 ½ laps to the mile. He was facing a strong opposition, including such well-known peds as Jem Bailey, George Mason and 'Choppy' Warburton. Warburton, who, at 46, was well past his prime, was holder of the British professional 20-mile record and a former holder of British amateur records at two, six and ten miles. For several years he had been coaching Britain's best cyclists.

Len took the lead from the lanky Warburton (who'd been given a five-lap start) at the half-way mark and ran out the winner by a lap from Charley Rowe, having covered a net distance of ten miles 67 yards. As regards Choppy Warburton, Len would have been sanguine about his prospects of beating a man nearly twice his age but nevertheless quietly thrilled to have crossed swords with such illustrious company. This was one of Choppy Warburton's last running races. Tragically, he would die of heart attack in Paris less than two years later.

The win at Bow was the perfect tonic for Len's next undertaking – a three-hour, go-as-you-please race at the same venue on 12 December 1892. A generous purse, with £10 going to the winner, attracted some 30 of the best-known peds from in and around London even though the entry fee was a hefty five shillings per person. Other famous names on the entry list included the aforementioned Jem Bailey, and Arthur Norris, 36, the former professional champion at ten miles and 20 miles.

In spite of the fact that, for once, it was a 'shilling gate', the venue was packed with a bumper crowd. Mr A. Barrett, the handicapper, had given Len a start of 9 ¾ laps, or 1 mile 872 yards, with the champion, Norris, at scratch. The champion set about his task with vigour, covering ten miles 810 yards in the first hour. However, it quickly became apparent that he had been out-handicapped, particularly as regards Len, who covered 10 ¼ miles in the first hour, just 370 yards fewer than Norris.

Discouraged by what was clearly an insurmountable task, Norris retired in the 14th mile. Even with Norris out of the picture, Len still had to contend with the tireless Jem Bailey, who had been given a start of

11½ laps and had been holding up well for a veteran of 41 years. With his sinewy legs eating up the ground in effortless fashion, Len covered 15 miles 207 yards in one-and-a-half hours and 19 miles 1495 yards in two hours.

After taking the lead from Bailey at two hours, he continued to set a blistering pace and left his rivals behind. With the outcome a foregone conclusion, the three remaining competitors on the track mutually agreed to stop well before the full three hours had expired. The promoter having given his consent for the race to conclude in this way, a pistol was fired after 2 hours 42 minutes and Len was awarded the first prize. He had amassed a net distance of 25 miles 487 yards in that time. This was the equivalent of 2 hours 40 minutes for 25 miles, a tremendous performance by the standards of the day.

What made it even more impressive was that it had been accomplished on a grass track not known for being conducive to fast running. Up to that point, only four men in history had run faster, albeit on cinders, which generally provided better going. *The Sportsman* commented, 'Of the winner more will undoubtedly be heard anon. He was apparently as fresh and full of running at the finish as he was at the beginning of the race.'

The sporting fraternity realised that in Len and Joe Hurst they had two highly marketable long-distance runners in the making. The brothers were approached by the 'East London Sporting Syndicate', an organisation run by a group of businessmen seeking to promote sporting events in East London. The E.L.S.S. held weekly meetings held at the 'White Hart' in Bethnal Green Road, and they offered to back the brothers in forthcoming races.

Len accepted this opportunity to become a full-time professional, but his brother was more reluctant to enter into such an arrangement. He preferred the security of a guaranteed wage packet to the vagaries of professional athletics and decided to stay semi-professional. Perhaps wisely so: Joe was a generous open-handed individual and had a 'soft touch' as far as money was concerned; it would have been easy for his winnings to slip through his fingers.

One of the first running promotions of the East London Sporting Syndicate was a six-day race for the championship of the world at the Excelsior Hall in Bethnal Green. It was a 'go-as-you-please' contest in which competitors could, as the name implies, walk or run as they chose for 12 hours per day.

Opened in 1890, the Excelsior Hall housed baths, a 34-yard swimming pool with a glass atrium and a gallery for spectators. The pool could be boarded over to host sporting events, political meetings, and such like, and the pool area was large enough to accommodate an 80-yard running track.

The syndicate was offering £85 in prize money and a handsome silver cup for the winner. A bumper entry was assured. Big-purse, multi-day events like this had become few and far between since the halcyon days of the 'Astley Belt' races bankrolled by the late Sir John Dugdale Astley.

Of the 35 names recorded on the programme, 28 faced the starter, making for very busy proceedings on the small indoor circuit. To provide a forgiving surface underfoot, the boarded track had been covered with soft tan bark, which held up well and afforded good shock absorption.

The race got under way before a full house on Monday, 20 February 1893 and ran daily from 11am to 11pm. On the first day of the big event hundreds of people milled into the hall to watch the race. By the end of the evening, the air was thick with cigarette and cigar smoke mixed with the pungent odour of sweat; hardly ideal conditions for an endurance race; however, the imposition of a smoking ban would have been unthinkable in those days.

Len made a promising start. When the call was given to stop at 11pm he was lying in second place, having covered 79 miles and 18 laps within the allotted time. The second day, however, found him struggling with an undisclosed 'injury'.

At the end of the day he was languishing in tenth place with a score of 118 miles and 6 laps and retired from the contest, unable to continue. In a case of contrasting fortunes, his brother Joe was running well and closed to within 15 miles of the leader, George Mason, on the fourth day of the contest. He, too, struggled with an injury on the fifth day, but rallied on the last day to secure the fifth prize of £7 7s, having covered an aggregate distance of 370 miles. Mason made sure of the first prize of £30 by amassing 403.8 miles. This would have been one of the best marks on record, just 11 miles shy of George Littlewood's mark, had the track not been remeasured afterwards and found to be 11 yards short per lap.

Len's first foray into multi-day racing had been a baptism of fire, as it were. This was an event where experience was key, but that could only be gained by trial and error.

The East London Sporting Syndicate, emboldened by the success of its six-day race, decided to promote another long-distance contest at the Excelsior Baths the following month. Aficionados of the sport praised their efforts to resuscitate the fallen fortunes of what used to be termed the 'wobbles' – so named after the rolling gait of the American Edward Payson Weston, the 'father' of the six-day race.

Their next promotion was a 30-mile handicap for £11 in prize money. The race was decided in conjunction with a seven-mile walking handicap for the benefit of Jack Hibberd – the well-known long-distance walker, who had fallen on hard times. In the pre-welfare state era those unable to support themselves were reliant on the charity of their brethren. It was either that, an unexpected windfall, or off to the dreaded workhouse.

There were only seven starters in the 30-mile handicap, but this was, if anything, an advantage for the runners as it meant that the track would be less congested. Len was the virtual scratch man, with six laps' start, while Joe had been given 14 laps. George Mason, despite having won the recent six-day race and being a former holder of the world professional record for 25 miles (2:36:34 in 1881), had been awarded a start of 24 laps.

The Hurst brothers set off at a fast clip and reduced the deficit quickly,

Joe covering 9¾ miles in the first hour and taking the lead at 11½ miles. Len found himself unable to make any inroads on his brother's start but was successful in overhauling the rest of the field. When 25¾ miles had been completed, the men agreed to stop. This, it was reported, did not affect the result in any way, and allowed the building to be closed at eleven o'clock, in accordance with agreement. Joe had covered exactly 25 miles in 3 hours 17 minutes, and Len a similar distance. Unfortunately, the venture ended in a loss of over £15 to Hibberd's well-meaning friends.

After a run of indifferent results, Len hit his stride again in late October 1893 when he won a four-mile handicap off 75 yards at the White Hart Grounds in a good time of 20:51.0.

Then, on 6 November, starting from scratch, he took third prize in a ten-mile handicap at a cold, windswept Bow Running Grounds in around 58:15. This was indeed a timely return to form, because he was committed to a match with A.E. Ware, of Camden Town, over 20 miles for a wager of £5 a-side.

The match was decided at Bow on 27 November. It was, as far as we know, Len's first actual sweepstakes match, as opposed to an open race for cash prizes. The modus operandi in those days was to visit the offices of *The Sporting Life* in London and deposit one's stake with the newspaper, which acted as the intermediary stakeholder.

Professional 20-mile matches had become a very rare occurrence. The last notable one had been when Arthur Norris defeated Edward Warner at Bow on 15 February 1886.

Len had conceded his opponent a quarter-mile start. He was reportedly in 'splendid' condition and attended by Jem Bailey and Arthur Norris. No sooner than the starter had fired his pistol, Len set about reducing his opponent's lead, completing the first mile in 5:21, two miles in 10:40 and three miles in 16:10.5. By the end of the fourth mile (21:35) he had already caught and passed Ware.

After covering five miles in 27:08, Len reeled off miles of 5:22, 5:53, 6:37, 5:59 and 5:54 to take him to ten miles in 57:03. When he was lapped for the second time, Ware chose retirement over the ignominy of further humiliation. After completing 12 miles in 1:08:38, Len was given permission to stop by his opponent's backers.

The following day, of course, he was back at the offices of *The Sporting Life* to collect his winnings. By deciding to run against A.E. Ware, however, Len had passed up the chance to participate in another six-day, go-as-you-please race at Excelsior Baths, where his brother Joe, among others, was competing for a first prize of £40 and a Championship Belt, which had been on display at the White Hart throughout the previous week. With the East London Sporting Syndicate offering £83 in prize money – a very large sum of money indeed – this was a golden opportunity missed.

Joe was attended by Jem Bailey, his 'guide, philosopher and friend'. With Len looking on, Joe took second place and £15 in prize money behind a resurgent Jack Hibberd, from Bethnal Green, who walked his way to a stunning victory over the runners.

On the last day of the contest a match had been arranged between Len and William Bealey over 20 miles for £10 a-side, but this had to be aborted when pedestrianism revealed its uglier side and certain persons motivated by pecuniary interests induced a crowd to swarm on the track and stop the competitors. All attempts to renew the contest were frustrated and ultimately the referee declared it void and ordered the men to the dressing room.

During the first half of the next season, 1894, Len had a run of mostly indifferent results, due, in part, to him being heavily handicapped. He was also finding it difficult to arrange matches on equitable terms. The second half of the season, however, brought an upturn in his fortunes.

On 10 June, starting from scratch, he ran second in a ten-mile handicap at the White Hart Grounds behind Ted Shepherd of Higham, who had been awarded a 550-yard start and won with 170 yards to spare. Len's time of around 55:10 was an exceptional performance, undoubtedly the fastest ten miler ever run on the furlong running track inside the rough-and-ready enclosure adjacent to the White Hart public house at Tottenham Hale.

Towards the end of the summer, Len finally came to terms with Guy Temple of Southwark to run ten miles for £30 at Brown's Grounds, Nunhead, on 22 October. Despite the large sum of money at stake, the match failed to attract more than about 150 spectators.

Temple, who was 5ft 7in and 21 years of age, was an up-and-coming talent, but did his chances no good by turning out in galoshes which afforded him little grip on the wet and slippery turf – a sign of inexperience. Hurst, sporting white drawers and a guernsey, had wisely elected to wear spikes, or 'running pumps' as they were then commonly known.

After tracking Temple for the first three miles, Len took the lead at the instruction of Jem Bailey and, gradually drawing away, won with the greatest of ease and by a margin of nearly 1,000 yards in 58:24.0.

A trip to the offices of *The Sporting Life* would, of course, have been his first order of business the next day.

That same week, the following public notice appeared in the 'Pedestrianism' section of *The Sporting Life*:

'EXCELSIOR BATHS, MANSFORD STREET, BETHNAL GREEN – A great Thirty Hours' Go-as-you-Please race, for the championship of the world, commencing Wednesday evening, November 14, and for three following days. First prize £15 and a championship silver belt; second prize, £8; third prize, £4; and £2 each for the next three covering over 150 miles. Entrance fee, 2s. 6d. Admission 6d, 1s, and 2s.'

Sure enough, the generous prize list generated a great deal of interest amongst peds in and around London. The promoting East London Sporting Syndicate had no option but to sift out the wheat from the chaff, since allowing too many runners to take part would have been counterproductive given the small size of the track.

Accordingly, all the chosen applicants had pedigree. Among those chasing the valuable prizes on offer were ex-champions George Hazael and George Mason.

The packed arena was abuzz with anticipation when the contest got under way at 8pm. The competitors would be asked to compete for three hours on the first day and nine hours on each of the other three days.

Celebrated Irish miler George Tincler, participating under his alias 'J. Craig of Inverness', looked dangerous for the first 12 miles but ran himself to a standstill after just two hours and retired. William Bealey, despite the handicap of having lost his left arm in a hunting accident, led at the end of the evening, having covered 25 miles 14 laps. The Hurst brothers were already well to the fore, Joe lying second with 25 miles and 12 laps; and Len third, with 25 miles and 7 laps.

All things considered – the bad air, the tight radii and the heavy pedestrian traffic – these were impressive performances.

Hazael, 50, a former holder of the 20-mile world record and the first man to run 600 miles in six days, plodded around steadily and racked up a respectable 20 miles and 19 laps. The old champion would, however, make his exit shortly after the contest resumed at 1pm, his aging legs being no longer able to withstand the punishment. Bealey paid for his extravagance on the previous evening; he was dispossessed of the lead after three hours by Len, who, in turn, was overhauled by a sprightly-looking Tommy Dance.

When the bell rang at 10pm to annunciate the end of the second session, Dance led with a score of 82 miles and 6 laps; Len was lying in second with 79 miles and 17 laps and his brother was third with 79 miles and 6 laps.

The penultimate day of the contest saw Len regain the lead and go into the final day in pole position, with a score of 135 miles and 12 laps; Dance was lying in second,with 134 miles and 8 laps, and Joe was lurking in third with 129 miles and 9 laps.

Only eight men were left in the race on the last day of the contest, the feature of which was the impressive running of Len's brother Joe, who swept into the lead at half past six in the evening. A seasoned campaigner, Joe was never headed thereafter and, covering an impressive 58 miles and 17 laps that day, swept to victory. Len, battling exhaustion, just managed to hold on to second place ahead of Tom Dance.

Result: 1. Joe Hurst 188 miles 6 laps; 2. Len Hurst 184 miles 16 laps; 3. Tommy Dance 183 miles

The attendance figures had been only moderate during the week but improved considerably on the last day, when the closeness of the contest prompted much wagering.

We were delighted to discover that, at the time of writing, the jewelled silver championship belt which Joe Hurst was awarded for winning this contest is still partially intact and in the safekeeping of a descendent. Today the belt is no longer complete, the fabric having either disintegrated or been removed, but the silver buckles and badges are all there. The mere existence of this valuable family heirloom can be attributed to the foresight of Joe, who left it to his daughter, Ada, rather than to one of his sons, safe in the knowledge that she would ensure its safekeeping.

Silver buckles from the championship belt awarded to Joe Hurst at Excelsior Hall in 1894.

For Len, the highlight of an otherwise uneventful 1895 season was a 20-hour, go-as-you-please race at the Excelsior Baths in Bethnal Green in early December. After dropping out in 1893 and snatching defeat from the jaws of victory in 1894, could he make it third time lucky?

As with previous such events at this venue, this one was again promoted by the East London Sporting Syndicate, who were offering £20 in prize money, but no championship belt, in return for an entrance fee of 2s 6d. The race was to extend over four nights of five hours each.

Only 11 peds submitted entries, others doubtless being deterred by the presence of the Hurst brothers.

With two of the original number having failed to appear, the starter, Mr J.T. Hulls, sent the runners on their way shortly after 5pm on Tuesday, 3 December. Len got off to a good start and, save for the second hour, when Joe was in front, led throughout the evening, covering 25 miles three laps in three hours and 38 miles eight laps at the conclusion of the fifth hour.

By the end of the evening the field had been whittled down to six men, Joe lying second, eight laps behind, and Tommy Dance third, with 36 miles nine laps.

The second day of the contest saw Len consolidate his lead by covering 23 miles eight laps in three hours and 36 miles at the expiration of time to take him 21 laps clear of his brother, with the field now down to five men. The arrival of the Excelsior Band later in the evening served to lighten up the proceedings under the gaze of a growing crowd of spectators.

The positions stayed unchanged on the third day, although Joe matched the entertainment provided by the band by slashing his brother's lead from 21 to 13 laps. Despite having to take intermittent walking breaks as fatigue set in, Len still managed to cover 34 miles, but after losing the previous year's race on the last day, and with Joe again poised to strike, Len was determined not to be denied on this occasion. This time he made sure of the victory by gaining 12 laps on Joe during the first two hours.

Having established a commanding lead, he did enough during the last three hours to keep his brother at arm's length; he could even afford the luxury of a seven-minute break. It had been a gruelling week, with four races of 30 or more miles in four consecutive days, culminating in a payday of £10.

Result: 1. Len Hurst 138 miles 15 laps; 2. Joe Hurst 136 miles 16 laps; 3. Tommy Dance 132 miles 13 laps

This was to be the last of the go-as-you-please running contests to be promoted by the East London Sporting Syndicate at the Excelsior Hall. A tell-tale sign had been the reduced prize money – a quarter of that which had been offered two years previously. A drop-off in attendance figures and betting revenues had made the venture unprofitable, unlike the syndicate's popular, albeit controversial, boxing promotions, which continued at the Excelsior Hall until they were banned in 1898.

THE GOLDEN YEARS

1896 was a milestone year for sport in general. It marked the genesis of the modern Olympic Movement, and, on a more personal level for Len Hurst, the turning point in his athletic career.

Professional long-distance racing in Britain had been at a low ebb for several years, with lucrative competitive opportunities few and far between. Len was faced with the dilemma of being at the peak of his physical powers but unable to find profitable races. The first half of the year had been quiet, save for a handful of four-mile races, which did not suit him as well as the long distances. The pick of his early season results would have been his showing in a four-mile sweepstakes scratch race at Nunhead on 3 April, where he finished second behind Harry Anstead and ahead of George Tincler in 20:34.

Then a golden opportunity presented itself: an invitation, issued through the Paris-based boxing impresario Fred Boon, to run in the inaugural *Le Petit Journal Marathon* in Paris for a substantial prize on Sunday, 19 July. The invitation had been extended to both Hurst brothers. All their expenses to and from Paris would be guaranteed.

The brothers, needless to say, seized the opportunity.

From North London, Paris was a ten-hour journey by train and by steamer via Newhaven, Dieppe and Rouen. The brothers arrived in Paris on the eve of the race in the company of Fred Boon, acting as their manager. Boon, who originally hailed from London, had been promoting professional boxing matches in Paris for several years and evidently had UK syndicate connections.

Paris, with its broad boulevards, schools, elaborately designed parks and grand architecture, was the inspiration for legions of students, intellectuals, writers, composers and artists. When Len Hurst first came here in 1896, the cityscape was dominated by a towering steel spire: the Eiffel Tower, completed in 1889, the tallest man-made structure in the world and a salient symbol of French aspiration.

For someone who'd never set foot on foreign soil before, it must have seemed an exotic adventure. France was undergoing a sporting metamorphosis and would soon step out of the shadows of Great Britain and the USA as a major sporting power.

One of the key figures in the French sporting nascence was an enterprising journalist named Pierre Giffard. Giffard, by bringing to bear his influence as editor-in-chief of *Le Petit Journal*, was a driving force behind the promotion of foot-racing in France. One of his first initiatives was a mammoth 380-kilometre go-as-you-please foot race from Paris to Belfort in 1892. The event attracted a phenomenal number of entries and had a huge starting field of 1,100 competitors, making it the world's first mass-participation road race.

No fewer than 380 of the starters completed the gruelling ten-day ordeal. Significantly, coverage of the race by *Le Petit Journal* led to a massive spike in the newspaper's circulation, paving the way for future newspaper-sponsored sporting promotions.

Four years later, the inaugural Summer Olympics in Athens would provide the spark of inspiration for Giffard's greatest initiative. The culmination of the Games had been the home victory of Greek runner Spyros Louis in the 40-kilometre road race from Marathon to Athens. It had been such a huge success that Giffard decided to replicate it in Paris. It was to become the world's first 'City Marathon', predating the famous Boston Marathon by some nine months.

Although editor of Le Vélo at the time, he organised the race on behalf of Le Petit Journal. To attract a quality field, Le Petit Journal offered prizes of 1,000, 500 and 300 francs. In the event of the winner breaking the world record, it was announced that the first prize would be doubled. The winner would also receive a work of art of equivalent value to the prize money.

No fewer than 281 professionals put their names forward. Most of the entries were, of course, from France but, as indicated, there was also some British interest.

Overcast skies greeted the competitors ahead of the scheduled 6am start. Parisians turned out in force to watch the race, such was the lure of sport before the advent of live broadcasting. The city streets around Porte-Maillot were jam-packed with spectators.

A motley assemblage of competitors, 191 in number, lined up for the start on the broad boulevard at Saint Maillot. Many had dressed especially for the occasion and were sporting brightly coloured shirts and hats, extravagant costumes and belts with buckles and jingling bells;

a few even carried walking canes; most were wearing stout shoes, but some were barefooted.

As a tribute to Greece, each of the runners wore a blue-and-white striped armband which displayed his starting number. Len's was 170.

To deter would-be cheats, there were several checkpoints, at which the runners were required to stop and sign in. Inevitably, given the sheer number of bystanders, there was a delay of several minutes until all the runners had been lined up in an orderly fashion and the road ahead cleared.

Finally, at ten past six, Pierre Giffard gave the command 'Un, deux, trois – allez', and the runners charged off amid loud cheering and waving.

The 40-kilometre course would take them on a winding route from Porte-Maillot to Conflans-Sainte-Honorine via Ville d'Avray, Versailles, Rocquencourt, Marly and Saint-Germain-en-Laye. In keeping with tradition, no pacers, be it on foot or on bicycle, were to be allowed. The largely unpaved road, it was later reported, was in very good condition, except at Marly, where the runners had to negotiate rough cobbles.

Henri Mathlin, the French champion, was the first to lead the way. Setting an ambitious pace, he built up a substantial lead during the first 10 kilometres. When he arrived at the checkpoint in Versailles, having covered the 16.8 kilometres up to that point in a very fast 1:00:37, he was still 200 metres ahead of Len. However, Len, having set off steadily, was already narrowing the gap. On the outskirts of Versailles, he caught and passed Mathlin, then immediately set about pressing home his advantage. On reaching Marly-le-Roi (25 km), he was already two minutes ahead of his nearest pursuer. However, Len was anything but alone, for he was surrounded by a swarm of cyclists, some 150 in number – the 1896 equivalent of live coverage.

On reaching the 29.5 kilometres checkpoint at Saint-Germain, in 1:49:05, he refreshed himself with a glass of freshly squeezed orange juice. Then, six kilometres later, he took a slug from a bottle of champagne as he approached Croix-de-Noailles. The drinking of champagne during a marathon race might, in this day and age, sound somewhat decadent, reckless even, but in those days the unchlorinated Parisian tap water was unfit for human consumption. Years later, the English novelist Arnold Bennett would famously die of typhoid two months after drinking a glass of water in a Paris hotel to prove it was safe.

Maintaining a relentless pace all the way to Conflans-Sainte-Honorine, Len was cheered home by a throng of some 2,000 spectators who had crammed on to the bridge over the River Seine, where the finish was marked by an official holding a pole with a sign reading 'Arrivée'.

Len barely had time to catch his breath in the arms of Mr Boon before being inundated with congratulators. His finishing time of 2:31:29.8 was intrinsically superior to George Dunning's track world record for 25 miles. The spectators had to wait fully six minutes until the next finisher, Victor Bagré, arrived.

Len's brother Joe acquitted himself well for a 'veteran' by moving up through the field to finish a creditable sixth in two hours 53 minutes. No

Paris, July 1896. Len Hurst and his manager Fred Boon.

fewer than 49 of the 81 finishers were awarded a commemorative medal by *Le Petit Journal* for beating four hours.

After the race, the runners received a medical check-up before returning to Paris by train for the awards ceremony, which was conducted at the offices of *Le Petit Journal*. True to their word, the organisers gave Len 2,000 francs for breaking the 'world record'. To give an idea of how much this was in relative terms, a copy of the *Le Petit Journal* cost five centimes. Joe finished outside the prize money but was awarded a special prize of 100 francs for bettering the time achieved by Spyridon Louis in Athens.

Len was the toast of Paris after his win. *Le Petit Journal* hailed it a 'triumph of physical strength and training … a prodigious effort.'

After the race, perhaps emboldened by the effect of the beer he was drinking, Len announced that he would return in a year's time to defend his title and better his winning time by five minutes. A week after taking Paris by storm, a lithograph of Len was featured on the front cover of the popular illustrated weekly supplement to *Le Petit Journal*. By then at the latest, he was a household name in the French capital.

The vanquished French runners were keen to regain their laurels. It was the French who had invented the word 'revenge' after all.

Len was immediately challenged to a one-hour running match by Henri Mathlin. The French champion was anxious to exact his revenge at a distance he believed favoured him, having led to Versailles in the marathon race. Hurst accepted on the condition that the stakes be no less than 500 francs and the match take place before 3 September.

Le Petit Journal

Le Petit Journal

Le Supplément illustré

SUPPLÉMENT ILLUSTRÉ

Huit pages : CINQ centimes

ABONNEMENTS

Septième année

DIMANCHE 2 AOUT 1896

Numéro 298

LA COURSE DE MARATHON
organisée par le « Petit Journal »

Paris, 2 August 1896: this lithography of Len Hurst winning the inaugural Paris-Conflans Marathon graced the cover of the illustrated supplement to Le Petit Journal.

43

A match was agreed upon and decided at the Buffalo Velodrome in Neuilly-sur-Seine on 1 August. The small and intimate velodrome, as immortalised in a painting by Henri de Toulouse-Lautrec, featured a 300-metre dirt running track on the infield.

At the sounding of a bell, both men stepped up to the starting line, Len sporting grey and blue and the same armlet he wore during the Paris-Conflans race. The two protagonists shook hands briefly, and then the starter dropped the flag to get the race under way. Mathlin immediately shot into the lead and opened a gap of 12 metres. However, Len had no intention of giving his rival a big head start this time and was at Mathlin's heels by the completion of four laps.

At the completion of the 12th lap, Len took the lead and picked up the pace, gaining a small gap on Mathlin, who doggedly gave chase. This was how it remained for 25 laps, when Mathlin stopped to change his shoes which, he complained, were hurting his feet.

Len, doubtless bewildered, ran on, but, after the spectators yelled for him to stop, he sportingly slowed down to let his opponent catch up. Five laps later, Mathlin was back on level terms, and the racing resumed.

The next injection of pace was enough to see off Mathlin. When the bell rang out at the completion of an hour, Len had covered 16,580 metres; two laps, or 600 metres, more than his opponent. By way of an encore, he kept going to complete 17 kilometres in 1:01:28 and set his third French record of the day. Despite having lost time hanging around for

Mathlin, Len established new French records for 5,000 metres (17:13.4) and 10,000 metres (35:41.6) en route to winning the race.

A day after returning to England, he competed in two events in the August Bank Holiday Sports in Sittingbourne, where, as the returning hero, he was, of course, the centre of attention. Despite all his recent exertions, not to mention the heavy travel, he overhauled the entire field to win the four-mile handicap from scratch in a fast time of 20:26.0.

A few days later, Len steamed back to Paris to face the former amateur French cross-country champion Alfred Chauvelot in a 20-kilometre handicap at the Buffalo Velodrome, having conceded the latter a generous start of 750 metres. Chauvelot, third-placer in the Paris-Conflans Marathon, had, in the run-up to the match, claimed he could defeat Hurst on equal terms, so, with the benefit of a generous start, he was the odds-on favourite to win.

The race, the culmination of a busy evening of cycling and foot racing, got under way at 9.45pm under darkening skies inside the well-illuminated velodrome. Len, realising he would have his work cut out to make up 750 metres on his opponent, set off in workmanlike fashion.

Despite his recent heavy racing schedule, he looked light on his feet as he rhythmically carved out the first 5 kilometres (16:58.8) and 10 kilometres (35:00.4) – both new French records. He had covered 16,612 metres at the completion of the hour – eclipsing Frantz Reichel's French record by a single metre – and finally caught Chauvelot during the 18th kilometre.

The Frenchman offered no response when Len went by, having clearly run himself out. With Chauvelot trailing in his wake, he eventually won with 150 metres to spare in yet another French record of 1:12:44.4. Having not won the Paris-Conflans Marathon Race but also defeated two French challengers, Len was the indisputable nemesis of France's professional foot-racing elite. For the time being at least.

Back in his native homeland, the tide also turned in Len's favour when several elite athletes were suspended by the A.A.A. ahead of the 1896 national championships on allegations that they had received payments declared as expenses.

Len would no doubt have been delighted to find out they banned wrongdoers included some of the world's finest amateur long-distance runners of the day: George Crossland, reigning A.A.A. ten miles and national cross-country champion and holder of outright world records for 20 miles and two hours; Fred Bacon, amateur world mile record holder and winner of A.A.A. titles at the mile in 1893, 1894 and 1895, four miles in 1894 and ten miles in 1896; and Harry Watkins, runner-up in the A.A.A. ten miles championship in 1894, 1895 and 1896.

The A.A.A., in its determination to make an example of system abusers, had resorted to the extreme measure of expelling its crème de la crème, even though it must have been conscious of the fact that by doing so it was giving pedestrianism a much-needed shot in the arm. The suspensions sent shockwaves through the amateur athletics world. The payment of expenses was subject to A.A.A. approval in those days, but expenses could be, and were, used to mask illicit appearance fees. That, however, was not the only area where abuses of the amateur code were rife.

While amateurs were prohibited from accepting prize money, meeting promoters could advertise the monetary value of the prizes on offer – typically goldware or silverware, which was easily convertible to cash. Messrs. Crossland, Watkins and Bacon appear through their actions to have crossed the proverbial line in the sand, forcing the A.A.A. to take draconian measures.

In Len Hurst's day it was not uncommon for amateurs to masquerade as professionals by competing under an alias; for some, the potential pecuniary rewards outweighed the risk of a lifetime ban if caught. In keeping with a social order that favoured the ruling classes, it is interesting to note that the law was less lenient for professionals who impersonated amateurs. In 1892 a pedestrian named Mellor was sentenced to a month's imprisonment for entering as an amateur in a mile handicap meeting at Sheffield, where he won a six-guinea timepiece.

Len, upon his return from France, seized the opportunity by declaring publicly that he was ready to 'run any man in the world from 20 to 30 miles level on either road or track.' This was, of course, a thinly veiled challenge to the amateur exiles who overnight had become his new-found rivals. The challenge to all-comers appeared to have the desired effect for both Crossland and Watkins expressed an immediate interest in meeting Hurst. Matches were proposed but, that year at least, they failed to materialise.

For Len, the 1897 season was shaping up to be another quiet one, with nothing to occasion him travelling to Paris. The Paris to Conflans Marathon Race had been discontinued after just one year, the promoting newspaper *Le Petit Journal* having announced that it had no ambitions to make the race an annual fixture.

At the start of the year, however, he entered his first, tentative negotiations with Harry Watkins. High-stakes matches were typically preceded by heavy correspondence, and this one was to prove no exception. Finally, in June, they agreed to run 20 miles for a huge sum of £200. It was the showdown the pedestrian world had been waiting for.

On 15 June Len warmed up for the task by running a 10-mile exhibition match against his brother Joe at the King's Head Grounds in Lower Edmonton. The 'track' was an ordinary garden path measuring 17 laps and 60 yards to the mile. Despite this handicap, Len won without turning a hair in 58:28.0 – much faster had been anticipated.

A few weeks before the race, Len had travelled to Southport to make his final preparations under the watchful eye of his backer and trainer, Mr. J.W. Turner, of Shrewsbury. Watkins did likewise at Blackpool, where he trained under the supervision of Fred Bacon, 'Sonny' Morton and George Crossland, the latter two being former and current holders, respectively, of the amateur 20-mile world record.

The highly anticipated match was decided at Ewood Park in Blackburn on Saturday, 24 July. The weather on the day was fine, if a little too muggy for record-breaking. However, a 'magnificent' cinder track had been prepared by the Blackburn Rovers groundsman. Moreover, both runners turned out in prime condition. In addition to deciding the 'Twenty Miles Championship of the World', an attempt would also be made to lower Crossland's formidable record of 1:51:54. A bumper crowd was assured.

There were about 4,000 people round the ropes when the referee gave the signal to start, more than an hour after the advertised time. Watkins was the 2:1 odds-on favourite, not least because of a glittering track career which had seen him setting world-beating marks of 14:31.0 for three miles, 30:25.0 for six miles and 51:40.0 for ten miles. The Coventry man had recently displayed great form when narrowly defeated by Fred Bacon over five miles in Liverpool in a fast time of 25:32.0. Crucially, however, his only previous racing experience at 20 miles had been a race which he had failed to finish three years earlier.

With his marathon running background, Len undoubtedly had the advantage in the endurance stakes and would have known that his best chance of winning lay in running the legs off his opponent. He took the lead straight away and wasted no time carving out a fast pace, ripping through the first mile in 5:07, two miles in 10:25, three miles in 15:47 and four miles in 21:17. In the early stages of the race it even seemed likely that the record would be beaten, but then Watkins took the lead and slowed the pace down.

Watkins lead through five miles in 26:58 and six miles in 32:40, but Len regained the lead at seven miles (38:34), with all prospects of a record gone. Len continued to lead the way until 10 miles (55:50), when he pulled up for a drink and allowed Watkins to slip by him. The Coventry man led at a more leisurely pace until the 12th mile when Len once more took up the running and threw in a fast 5:32 mile; however, it was insufficient to dispose of Watkins.

At 13 miles Len stopped again to take a pull at a bottle, but he caught Watkins like a shot, then, in an unabashed display of gamesmanship, reclaimed the lead amid loud cheers and laughter. The general opinion was still that Watkins would win as he liked, but soon the pace Len had been setting began to have a telling effect on his rival, who was seen to be grimacing in discomfort at 14½ miles.

Then, with a suddenness that brought gasps from the crowd, Watkins broke down and a yawning gap immediately appeared as Len streaked away. The Coventry man was nearly half a lap behind when he pulled up 20 yards short of 15 miles and left the track nursing what appeared to be a bad leg.

Len completed 15 miles in 1:25:43 and, keeping on, did 15¼ miles in 1:27:12 when the Watkins party indicated that he need not complete the full 20 miles. Despite the humidity, Len finished looking fresh as paint. As he left the track, he entertained the crowd with a spectacular somersault, such, no doubt, was his delight at a £200 payday. The outcome of the match had been something of a turn-up for the books, with most of the punters going home somewhat the poorer. Few had genuinely expected him to win, let alone so comprehensively.

Having defeated Watkins, Len was still keen to meet Crossland that year, but was palpably frustrated by the Stalybridge runner's reticence. In

August the *Freeman's Journal* revealed why: 'After his defeat of Watkins, Hurst has challenged all-comers to run a twenty miles race for £100 or £200 aside. He pointedly remarks that Crossland, present holder of the twenty miles record, ought to accept his challenge. He also states his willingness to meet Crossland in a series of matches, viz. – ten, fifteen, and twenty miles, for a substantial purse. The latter, however, is altogether out of training at present.'

By the autumn, however, Crossland was back in training and ready to negotiate. In late October they agreed to a 10-mile race at Rochdale Athletic Grounds on Saturday, 5 February for £200.

The victory over Watkins was not the only milestone event that year. Wedding bells were also ringing for Len, who was married to Caroline

Ewood Park, Blackburn, 1897: Harry Watkins (left of centre) and Len Hurst (right of centre), pictured before their match for the 20-mile Championship of the World.

Ethel Munro, an accountant's daughter five years his junior, in a Protestant ceremony at West Ham. They settled into a terraced house adjacent to Ethel's parents in Bury Street, Edmonton, a stone's throw from the Edmonton brick fields. A year later, Ethel gave birth to their first child, a boy, whom they named Leonard. They would have three more children: Elsie in 1900; Fred in 1901; and, finally, Alfred in 1909.

The 1898 season saw Len in heavy training right from the outset. In mid-January, three weeks before his match against George Crossland, he arrived at the residence of his backer, Mr Turner, and commenced his final preparations under the care of the same at the Southport Athletic Society's Grounds.

Crossland, meanwhile, was putting the finishing touches to his training at Morecambe under the supervision of the great Scottish professional Willie Cummings, who then was still the holder of the professional world record for ten miles. As an amateur competing in the colours of Salford Harriers and latterly Manchester Harriers, he had been a winner of the English National Cross-Country Championship in 1894 and 1896 and the A.A.A. ten-mile championship in 1896. He was also still the holder of the English four-mile record (19:28.6) and the world 20-mile record (1:51:54). His 20-mile mark dating from 1894 was far superior to anything that had previously been accomplished by a professional, a fact Len would have been acutely aware of, hence his rigorous preparations at Southport. Crossland, though, had struggled to rediscover his form since his suspension. Sensing another upset, the bookies made Len their favourite at 5-4 on.

George Crossland.

Some 5,000 spectators had turned out to watch the race. Among the faces in the crowd were numerous athletics stars past and present, including Bill Lang, Jimmy Nuttall, 'Treacle' Sanderson, Edward Parry, Harry Watkins and Fred Bacon. After some initial theatrics, Crossland led through a mile in 5:19 and two miles in 10:20. Running with an elastic stride, Len was content to let Crossland cut out the early work before easing ahead just before the completion of three miles in 15:42.5.

The quarter-mile cinder track was in excellent condition for this time of year. As a front runner, Crossland was ahead again within two laps and led through four miles in 21:09, five miles in 26:42.4 and six miles in 32:07. Then, at six miles, Len spurted past Crossland and suddenly a three-yard gap appeared. The Stalybridge man managed at first to hold the gap but was unable to sustain the effort and, much to the disappointment of his numerous supporters, pulled up just before 6½ miles.

With no opponent to press him, Len ran on to the finish, his time for the ten miles being 54:02.5. A crowd-pleasing last lap of 1:12.5 proved that he could have run faster had he been pushed. He had added yet another major 'scalp' to his burgeoning collection but would hardly have expected to have dispatched Crossland with such ease.

His next opponent would prove a different proposition altogether. On Saturday, 19 March 1898 he took on Irish champion Jack Mullen over five miles for £50 a-side and an equal share of the gate money at the City and Suburban Grounds in Dublin.

Mullen, 29, was the Irish amateur record holder for one, two and five miles, and a former champion of Ireland at the half mile, mile, four miles, five miles and cross-country. On 13 September 1894, with a 100-yard start, he had famously defeated Fred Bacon by more than his starting allowance at Belfast in an Irish record of 25:21.0.

For a marathon runner such as Len, a mere five miles was well below his best distance. Under the terms of the contest, however, he knew he would not be leaving the Irish capital empty handed whatever the outcome. He arrived in Dublin by steamer three days before in the company of his backer, J.W. Turner. The following day he visited Jones's Road with Mullen and indulged in a 'warm-up', where, it was reported, he put in some impressive running.

On the Saturday, a large crowd of 10,000 spectators turned out in fine spring weather to watch their man race the 20-mile Champion of the World. Despite setting a fast pace in the early stages of the race, Len was unable to shake off Mullen, who also took turns at leading. The lead swung back and forth, neither man gaining an advantage. Then, as the bell rang out, Len surged past his opponent and launched a long run for home.

However, Mullen stalked his prey with predatory ease and 200 yards from the finish unleashed a blistering sprint which carried him to victory by 45 yards in 25:50.0. It had been patently clear that Len did not have the tools in his armoury to outrun Mullen over such a short distance, let alone live with the Irishman's renowned finish.

The following week, *Pearson's Athletic Record*, a short-lived sporting journal of the period, commented dismissively, 'Few people could have supposed that Leonard Hurst had any chance against so speedy a man as J.J. Mullen over so short a distance as five miles. It is doubtful whether Hurst himself thought much of his prospects – beyond getting a substantial share of gate money.'

Len, like any professional worth his salt, hated losing. When all was said and done, however, he raced to feed and clothe his family, and with that responsibility came the pragmatic insight that the end sometimes justified the means. After losing to Mullen, Len was approached by the directors of the Bolton Wanderers Football Club, who invited him to come to their ground and launch an assault on George Crossland's 20-mile world record. They offered him the sum of £100 plus half gate receipts if he succeeded and £100 in the event of failure.

By offering such an incentive, they of course had no difficulty in getting Len to agree to attempt the feat. The run had originally been scheduled for Easter Monday but heavy rain had left the Burnden Park track waterlogged and unsuitable for fast running. Len eventually agreed to postpone the run to Saturday, 16 April 1898 for a consideration of £30 to cover his additional expenses. The arrangement guaranteed him £130, which is equivalent to about £12,000 in today's money.

He again finalised his preparations at Southport and was reported to be 'in the pink' when he toed the starting line in near windless conditions on a sunny Saturday afternoon. The attendance was, however, very disappointing – much smaller than had been anticipated. Only 771 paying spectators passed through the turnstiles, far too few for Bolton Wanderers to turn a profit.

Spectators included Fred Bacon, George Crossland and Harry Watkins, together with his trainer Sonny Morton, the latter himself a former holder of the amateur 20-mile record, having run the distance in 1:52:51.2 at Stamford Bridge in 1890.

To ensure the legitimacy of the result, the esteemed J.H. 'Harry' Hardwick, founder of Salford Harriers, officiated as a referee and timekeeper. The square-shaped cinder track around the football pitch was 397 yards 2ft in circumference, which meant that 88 laps 205 yards 1ft had to be covered in order to complete the full 20 miles.

Len had as pacemakers a Southport friend on a bicycle and his brother, Joe, and Harry Anstead, the two peds taking alternate turns to run a lap.

From the start, Len was inside record pace, reeling off the first ten miles in 54:16, eight seconds quicker than Crossland during his record-breaking run, and 11 miles 60 yards in the first hour.

His intermediate times at 13 miles (1:10:56) and 14 miles (1:16:38) were the fastest on record by a professional.

His 15-mile time of 1:22:21 was fewer than six seconds slower than Sid Thomas's amateur record and fully 50 seconds faster than Crossland during his record-breaking run. It was not the fastest on record by a professional, though, that distinction belonging to William 'The American Deer' Jackson (William Howitt), who had been credited with a time of 'one hour and twenty-two minutes' at the Copenhagen House ground, Islington, on 29 March 1852.

A 5:53 mile took Len to 16 miles in 1:28:14, 32 seconds faster than Crossland, and a new world record. Although his pace slipped to just outside six minutes for the first time, his 17-mile split of 1:34:15 was another world record, eight seconds faster than Crossland. In the 18th mile, however, he slowed dramatically as the pace began to exact its price, and in the 19th, despite the best efforts of his assistants and the exhortations of his supporters, Len lost well over a minute on Crossland's record, and all hope of a record was lost. It was now a question of whether he would last the distance and thus secure the £100 guaranteed, conditional on him completing the full 20 miles.

He did so, fortunately, albeit under 'distressing circumstances'. Finally, over three minutes after the record had been missed, he dragged his exhausted frame past the finishing post. The time officially recorded for the full distance was 1:55:33, but in those last three miles he had experienced the dreaded moment every marathon runner fears most – he had 'hit the wall'. He was so exhausted, he had to be carried to the dressing room by his attendants.

The *Evening Express* summed it up thus: 'Leonard Hurst, in his attack on the twenty miles record at Burnden Park, made the fatal mistake, so frequently committed, of forcing the pace too much at the outset.'

He would have gained some consolation, however, in the fact that his time was a new British professional record, supplanting the 1:56:38 set by the late

James 'Choppy' Warburton at Blackburn on 7 May 1880. It was arguably the best mark on record by a professional; Private Patrick Byrnes of the 101st Regiment (Canada) had reportedly clocked one hour 54 minutes at Halifax, Nova Scotia, on 4 October 1879, but there was some doubt over this mark as Byrnes lacked the credentials. Bacon, Crossland and Watkins each in turn issued him a challenge; Watkins, it was reported, presenting the strongest case. Len, however, intimated that he would be taking a month's rest before committing to a match against any of these men.

This would, however, have to wait a little longer because there was good news from Paris, where *l'Auto* magazine had announced it would be reviving the Paris to Conflans Marathon Race after a year's hiatus. The date of the race had been set for Sunday, 26 June. Len arrived in Paris in the company of his brother, Joe, and an entourage which reportedly consisted of Henry J. Marse of the *Sporting Life*; Herbert Woodcraft, his new manager; Arthur Hills and Walter Evans, his sponsors; and James Holcombe and William Legras, his trainers.

The Hurst brothers were two of four Britons in the field of 59 professionals who set off on their 40-kilometre journey from Porte-Maillot in cold and rainy weather at six o'clock in the morning.

The going was heavy, the roads being in bad condition with mud and dirt. Albert Charbonnel made the pace in the early stages of the race, reaching the 16.8-kilometre checkpoint at Versailles in a fast 59:30, closely followed by Filliet (59:33), Francois Champion (59:34), Len Hurst (59:35) and his brother Joe (59:45).

Shortly after leaving Versailles, Charbonnel was passed by Francois Champion. The young Frenchman, holder of national records from 1,500 metres to the one-hour run, then broke away. Meanwhile Len had lost his pacers, one owing to a punctured tyre. His shoes were torn to shreds by the sharp stones washed up by the rain, and his feet were bleeding.

A huge crowd numbering some 20,000 spectators cheered Champion past the 29.7-kilometre checkpoint at Saint-Germain in 1h 45min. He was 45 seconds ahead of Len, who, in turn, was followed by Charbonnel (1h 47min), Filliet (1h 50min) and Joe (1h 52min).

The question now was whether Len could repeat his feat of 1896, when, it will be recalled, he ran down the leader, Bagré, at halfway and won with minutes to spare. Sure enough, he started to reel Champion in and was just 20 yards behind the leader when he had to pull up at the railway crossing, some two kilometres from the finish. The subsequent effort to regain his lost ground brought on an attack of cramp, which forced him to stop briefly, and Champion won with ease in a course record of 2:30:10.

Len secured the F2500 second prize in 2:32:05, while his 41-year-old sibling rolled back the years to finish third in 2:45:00. Len, having lost the race under what he would have considered unlucky circumstances, immediately challenged the winner to run the same distance for a sum from £500 to £1,000. However, no response was forthcoming, the Frenchman's backers unable to match these terms.

A month after his return from Paris, a mile handicap at O'Ryan's Field in Ponder's End saw Len competing against a field that included not one but two of his brothers. Running off scratch, he had the measure of the field by the start of the last lap but graciously slowed down enough to allow his younger sibling Teddy to win.

After recovering from the gruelling Paris Marathon, Len was keen to renew his rivalry with George Crossland. However, Crossland, after his earlier defeat at Rochdale, initially had some difficulty in finding a backer to put up the requisite £100 until eventually music hall entertainer Alfred Saker came forward with the money. Len, it was reported, also had a new backer.

They agreed to run a ten-mile match for £200 at the Athletic Ground, Ashton-under-Lyne, on 27 August 1898. Both protagonists went about their usual pre-race preparations. For two weeks, Len trained alternately at Blackpool and Southport under the scrutiny of his old trainer Jack 'the referee' Taylor. Crossland did his build-up at Burbage near Buxton.

The Ashton Athletic Ground had a quarter-mile track that had been built specifically for cycle racing, being banked all round and surfaced with a red-brick dust. The weather on the day of the race was dull and gloomy, rain having fallen throughout most of the day. The track was sodden, pools of water lying near the edge, forcing the runners to go wide. The inclement weather also conspired to keep the gate down, with scarcely more than 800 people attending – far fewer than had been hoped for.

When they went to the mark, Len was the bookies' favourite at 11 to 8 on. Fred Bacon sent them on their way and Crossland, as was his custom, went straight to the front and made the running; he sped through the first mile in 5:05 with Len at his heels and looking confident.

Then the rain started to pour, causing the condition of the track to deteriorate with every successive lap. With the Stalybridge runner making the pace, they covered two miles in 10:25, three miles in 15:51, four miles in 21:22 and five miles in 26:50.

The next mile saw Len begin to assert himself after a short exchange, and the change quickly began to tell on Crossland, who only managed with great effort to stay at Len's shoulder through six miles in 32:14. However, Crossland was only able to stay with Len for another lap before giving up. Stalybridge's famous son cut a dejected figure as he hobbled off to the dressing room.

Len was duly told about a furlong from the finish of the seventh mile that he could stop when he pleased. He smiled cheerfully and put on a fine sprint to complete the seven miles in 37:50 and then called it a day. The *Illustrated Police News*, one of the earliest British tabloids, using a war metaphor, called it 'a bloodless victory' over Crossland.

Even before the Crossland match, Len's next match had already been arranged. It would be an attempt on the 15-mile world record at the Memorial Grounds in Canning Town on Saturday, 10 September 1898. The Memorial Grounds were the home of Thames Ironworks Football Club, who later became West Ham United. Opened to commemorate

Queen Victoria's Diamond Jubilee in June 1897, this 'sports complex' boasted Britain's longest swimming pool, a football pitch, a cycle track with the highest banking in the country and a three-lap cinder running track.

A crowd of 1,000 spectators turned out in less-than-ideal conditions, with a biting wind sweeping across the stadium. Paced by the same cyclist/runner team as at Bolton earlier in the year, Len got off to a good start and had the record firmly within his sights, cranking out the first five miles in 26:52.0. However, the next five miles saw his pace drop off as the heavy track and wind began to take their toll. By the time he had covered ten miles – in 54:45.2 – the record had already slipped from his grasp. Not wanting to disappoint the crowd, though, he kept going to complete the full distance in a time of 1:23:08.2. It was one of the fastest times on record, and a performance which the *Morning Post* lauded as 'one of considerable merit'.

In the days after his failed world record attempt at Canning Town, Len finally came to an agreement with Fred Bacon. In London they signed articles for two matches to decide the 'Long Distance Championship of Great Britain'. The first match was to be over ten miles and the second over 15 miles. The distances had been agreed upon by both parties in the interests of a balanced and fair contest, ten miles being Bacon's favoured distance and 15 miles being better suited to Len. Each race carried a purse of £100, so that in addition to the championship, a considerable sum of money was at stake.

The first match, ten miles on level terms, was decided at the Ashton-under-Lyne Athletic Grounds on Saturday, 8 October 1898. A large crowd numbering about 5,000 persons turned out in glorious weather to view the spectacle. When the news leaked that Len had caught a slight cold, Bacon was quickly installed 3 to 1 on favourite. Len, showing no apparent signs of weakness, led through the first mile in 5:15 and two miles in 10:36, before Bacon nimbly took over the pacing duties.

'The style shown by both men,' wrote the *Mid Surrey Times*, 'was similar, and the length of stride about the same in each case, but Bacon ran in a more graceful manner.'

By the completion of the fifth mile, in 26:48, Len was back in front and leading by a yard. The second half of the race continued in the same vein, with both men appearing to be running well within themselves. Len had probably sensed that he could not rid himself of Bacon, who, as one of the world's fastest finishers, was happy to sit and wait.

They raced round most of the last lap neck and neck, but the former A.A.A. mile champion was not to be denied and, edging ahead 20 yards from the finish, won a close race by a yard in 54:43.0. Nineteen days later, Len and Bacon decided the second match for the Championship at Rochdale, when, despite the drizzling rain, fully 3,000 spectators assembled at the Milnrow Road Athletic Grounds.

Both men appeared in good condition, Bacon having trained at Stockport in the company of his old rival George Crossland. Len had, once again, finished his preparation with three days of training at

Southport under the watchful eye of his mentor Jack Taylor. This time, Len was the bookies' favourite at 4 to 1 on.

Harry Watkins, acting as the starter, sent the men on their way shortly before four o'clock in the afternoon. Both men seemed keen to make an honest race of it and took alternate turns at setting the pace. At half way, Bacon looked untroubled as he led by a yard in a 40:11.6, emboldening the betting fraternity to hazard a wager on Bacon.

Three laps after leading through ten miles in 54:59.2, Len, owing to the onset of cramp, had to stop for treatment, and promptly found himself trailing Bacon by 50 yards. After a speedy rubdown by his trainer, however, he shot after Bacon and was back at the latter's shoulder by the end of the 12th mile. They were now outside Bacon's comfort zone and inside Len's.

As if on cue, Bacon started to show signs of distress in the 13th mile, allowing Len to open a gap on his rival despite a slower 5:54 mile split. Then, with a mile to go, Bacon stepped off the track complaining of a stitch. Though victory was assured, Len kept going to complete the full distance in another excellent time of 1:23:18. With the scores standing at one win apiece, the 'championship' was undecided, so the prospect of future matches or a decider in some shape or form looked a likely one.

Aside from the legendary Ranelagh Harrier Sid Thomas, Len was, subject to correction, the only athlete of his era to have defeated Fred Bacon, George Crossland and Harry Watkins in a track race on level terms. The aforementioned Sid Thomas was, incidentally, also suspended

Fred Bacon.

by the A.A.A. in 1896 over alleged expenses-related irregularities and afterwards turned professional, albeit without much success.

Len concluded an eventful 1898 season with a ten-mile match against Harry Watkins for £50 a-side at Rochdale Athletic Grounds on Saturday, 17 December. The Coventry man had made his final preparations at Blackpool and was reportedly in great form and keen to exact his revenge on Len for his earlier defeat over 20 miles.

Len had once again sought out the help of his old mentor Jack Taylor at Southport and was likewise fit and healthy. The weather was, however, miserable, the enclosure being enveloped in so much mist, it looked as though it would be impossible to run the race. However, both men were set on deciding the issue and insisted that the race went ahead.

Watkins immediately stamped his authority on the proceedings with a breath-taking 4:44 opening mile, which Len was unable to follow. A 5:00 second mile saw Watkins extend his lead to 150 yards at two miles. Running with a beautiful action, the Coventry man had exactly half a lap in hand at 3½ miles and over 300 yards at five miles, which he completed in 25:10.

Although Watkins gained very little in the next mile, no one was surprised to see Len step off the track at 6¼ miles. The race had lost its interest, and, no doubt, Len would have wanted to avoid the ignominy of being lapped. Watkins ran on for another quarter of a mile, then stopped after covering 6¾ miles in 34:18.4. It had to be acknowledged that at distances up to ten miles, Watkins was in a different league.

Pearson's Athletic Record observed, 'It is no coincidence that both Hurst and Watkins, like many other good stayers, adopt the lean-forward style of running.'

Summing up, the 1898 season had been a busy one with its ups and downs. By setting his first British and world track records, Len had also begun to fulfil the potential has elder sibling had seen in him as a youth.

In late December 1898, he turned 27 – a prime age for a long-distance runner. Few professional runners were blessed with a long career in this era. Health permitting, he would be able to maintain this level for a few more years. Long before the advent of antibiotics, the spectre of bacterial disease hung like a sword of Damocles over sportsmen such as Len Hurst. Tuberculosis, the big killer of the 19th and early 20th centuries, would claim, among thousands of others, the life of his great rival George Crossland in 1914.

The year 1899 marked the end of a transformative century and a decade capped by such pioneering advancements as the electric train, the Eastman Kodak camera, moving pictures and the diesel engine; advancements that would play a major role in shaping the 20th century. The relentless march of progress was transforming every sector of industry, including, of course, the brickmaking trade. A new, mechanised brickmaking process meant the days of the old-time brickmaker were numbered.

Since becoming a full-time professional, brickmaking had become a stopgap for Len – a secondary source of income during lean periods. He would eventually have to seek an alternative form of gainful employment after his retirement from competition. For the time being, though, he would continue to earn his living as a professional runner. He was a rare breed – one of only a handful of full-time athletes.

Len opened his account with a few low-key races before renewing his rivalry with Fred Bacon in a six-mile match for £100 at Lexden Park, Colchester, on 10 June 1899. Once again, Bacon timed his sprint finish perfectly to win by a yard in 32:18.0. He was appropriately dissatisfied with his performance, and promptly challenged Bacon to a rematch, which was decided a fortnight later at the Finney Gardens Athletic Grounds in Hanley, Staffordshire. Details of this match are sparse, save that it was run over ten miles for £50 a-side before 1,500 spectators, and that Len broke away in the last mile to win by 15 yards and turn the tables on Bacon.

Apart from the gruelling 15-mile match at Rochdale, their matches appear to have been orchestrated to have a close outcome. It looked suspiciously as though their scheme was to keep the issue finely balanced in order to keep the public interested. Clearly, this 'scam' could only go on for so long.

In early July, Len returned to France to contest the Paris-Conflans race, which had become an annual fixture. Apart from himself, the only other British entrant was Ted Shepherd, the self-styled 'Professional Champion of Kent'; a title Len himself would no doubt have coveted.

On Sunday, 2 July – race day – Len rose early on a dull and miserable morning and had a light breakfast. At around 5am, together with his mentor, Jack Taylor, and his Paris-based manager Mr Boon, he made his way to the Restaurant Gillet at Porte-Maillot to sign in and pick up his number (an armband). In all, 47 men came forward. The billiard room was recommissioned as a dressing room and massage saloon, the air thick with the odours of rubbing alcohol, Eau de Cologne and embrocation as the runners went about their pre-race rituals. Shortly before the 6am start, Mr Paul Rousseau, editor-in-chief of Le Vélo, came in and ordered the men to line up in front of the restaurant, before sending them on their way in front of the usual large crowd of spectators.

Two young French runners, Edmond Langlois and Jules Desgrandchamps, raced into an early lead. However, a chasing pack which included all the favourites kept them in their sights. At the Versailles checkpoint (16.8 kilometres) the order was: 1:00:30 Langlois, 1:01:00 Desgranchamps; 1:01:30 Cheminel, Hurst, Charbonnel and Shepherd; 1:02:00 Pottemain. The chasers eventually reeled in the early leaders; first Desgranchamps at Rocquencourt, and then Langlois on the outskirts of Marly. The roads having dried up, the race was heating up now. As Len had probably expected, it came down to a battle between himself and three-time French cross-country champion Albert Charbonnel. Both men were already clear of the field by around 20 kilometres and still running neck and neck at Saint-Germain (29.7 kilometres), where the positions were: 1:52:00 Charbonnel and Hurst, 1:53:00 Desgranchamps, 1:55:00 Shepherd, 1:58:00 Pottemain, 1:59:00 Langlois and Louyt. It was on the road to Conflans where the Frenchman, after receiving a stimulant, broke the deadlock with a decisive move to which Len was unable to respond. Running with a light, pitter-patter stride which was deceptively fast, Charbonnel ultimately ran out a comfortable winner in 2:33:10. Len, when he saw that his rival was not going to wilt, eased up on the run in to the finish and came in at a leisurely pace two minutes later in 2:35:12. As in the previous year, he was awarded F2,500 in prize money, then worth £12. Such was the dominance of the first two men, the third man home, Desgranchamps, was a mile in arrears. Ted Shepherd, who had started too quickly, struggled home in ninth in 2:57:00.

A couple of weeks after Paris *The Sporting Life* announced that Len would be making another attempt to beat George Crossland's 20-mile record at the Catford Sports Ground on 31 July. This was, apparently, in response to an offer made by a Mr George Thurling of Smithfield Market. Thurling, a well-known promoter of whippet handicaps, had promised to pay Len £25 should he succeed. Len was to be allowed any number of pace-makers during the race, on the condition that not more than three be on the track at the same time. While pace-making was frowned upon in amateur circles, professionals considered it legitimate in races against the clock. To help him accomplish his goal, Len recruited the assistance of Fred Bacon, Alf Griffin, Ted Shepherd, Alf Perkins and F. Thirkwell. Mr R. Watson was referee and took the times with a chronometer by reputed watchmaker Kendal & Dent.

The track was in good condition but there was the mitigating circumstance of a strong wind blowing down the back straight. The

Paris, 2 July 1899. The starting line-up for the third running of the Paris-Conflans Marathon. Len is second from the left.

betting started at '6 to 4 on time', the odds being against Len breaking the record. Despite the record billing, the attendance was dismal. Undaunted by the bad weather and lack of crowd support, Len set off at a record pace, covering the first mile in 5:16.5. Bacon was his first companion, Perkins on his bike pedalling by the side of him. After two and half miles Bacon stopped, leaving Griffin to take up the running, Perkins handing refreshments from the bicycle. In the fifth mile Griffin was relieved of his duties by Shepherd, who paced Len through five miles in 27:17.0 and six miles in 32:57¼. After Len had gone six miles, however, his pace dropped off. He soldiered on for another seven miles but had to abandon all hope of a record by ten miles (56:25.0) and aborted the mission after covering 13 miles 1,100 yards in 1:20:05. There was, of course, no legislating against the vagaries of the Great British weather, but it appears that the record was never really in peril. With the benefit of hindsight, Len might have conceded that he had needed more time to regain his full strength after the Paris Marathon four weeks earlier.

The following weekend, having recovered well from his exertions at Catford, he turned out in front of 14,000 spectators in a ten-mile scratch race at the August Bank Holiday Fete and Sports in his home town of Sittingbourne. The field consisted of only four starters: Len and his brother Joe, Fred Bacon and Harry Watkins, none of the local runners being game enough to face the 'big guns'. They were competing for prizes of £20, £6, £2 and £1. The fete at Gore Court Park had featured, among other things, boxing fights, fireworks and a spectacular balloon ascent and parachute drop from several thousand feet by Professor Fleet. However, the ten-mile race was the main attraction which most people had come to see. The six-lap grass track was in perfect condition, auguring well for a fast time. This certainly seemed to be on the cards when Watkins blazed through the first mile in a shade under five minutes, Len wisely making no attempt to go with the Coventry man. After just a mile, Bacon retired, owing to one of his ankles troubling him. Watkins reeled off the first four miles in 20:20.0, and by the completion of 4½ miles he was at Len's shoulders. Rather than lap his rival, however, Watkins was content to sit in and allow Len to dictate the pace. This was perhaps all part of a preordained plan, because Len responded by increasing his pace. Watkins, who was no doubt looking for a hard workout ahead of his upcoming attempt on the world's hour record, was operating at a record pace. Drafting in Len's wake, he covered five miles in 25:24.0, six miles in 30:33.0 and seven miles in 35:43.0. However, all hopes of a new world record were dashed when the pace slumped in the eighth mile. Two laps from home, Watkins unleashed an impressive finishing spurt which carried him to victory by a lap and more than the length of the straight. His time of 52:05.0 was less than a minute outside Willie Cummings's world record of 51:06.6. No time was reported for Len, who finished about quarter of a mile behind Watkins. However, we have it on authority from the late Alf Hurst that Len's personal best for ten miles was 53:28.0, and the evidence would suggest that he set it here in rural Sittingbourne against Harry Watkins and Fred Bacon.

To be a successful professional athlete during this era, it was important to establish and maintain amicable and reciprocal relations with one's peers, who were both rivals and business associates alike. It was a common practice among professionals to 'share the spoils', as it were. The great Scottish sprinter Alf Downer, in his autobiography entitled *Running Recollections and How to Train*, wrote, 'The best known "peds", as a rule, "stand in" with one another, which means they agree to divide among themselves any prize-money the school may win.' This would have doubtless been the case with Len Hurst, Harry Watkins and Fred Bacon. In order to stay afloat financially, professional runners were dependent on credible opposition and so saw it in their best mutual interests to support one another in his endeavours.

A month after his match against Watkins at Sittingbourne, Len returned the favour by making the long trip up to Rochdale to assist the Coventry ped in his attempt on the world's hour record. The record had been set by Fred Bacon on the same track on 19 June 1897, and stood at a formidable 11 miles 1,243 yards. The pace-making duties were to be shared by Len, Jack Walsh, the former Salford and Manchester Harrier; ace Scottish miler Alex Haddow, of East Calder; and Harry Brown, the well-known cyclist. Watkins had made his preparations at the seaside resort of Blackpool under the watchful eye of Jack Crossley, who had put his charge through a strict training regimen which had included walking 25 miles a day. In a private trial he had unofficially broken the world record for five miles. After a blustery and wet morning, the clouds lifted over the Rochdale Athletic Grounds, where the runners were welcomed by an enthusiastic crowd of 5,000 spectators. The three runners took it in turns to lead out Watkins, who, according to the *Coventry Herald*, 'ran well up behind the back wheel to take as much of the shelter as he could.' Len held up his part of the deal by shouldering much of the pace-making work in windy conditions ill-suited to record breaking. Working as a team, the pacers kept Watkins ahead of schedule, taking him through six miles in a world-leading 30:21.0, ten miles in 51:05.2 (world record) and 11 miles in 56:18.4 (world record). Bacon, during his record-breaking run, had passed ten miles in 51:11.0 and 11 miles in 56:28.0 before producing a great finishing spurt. Watkins was not to be denied, however, and pulled out a similarly strong finish to eclipse the record by 43 yards, and achieve a lifelong ambition.

An undisclosed illness would keep Len out of circulation for much of the remainder of the year, although in the early winter he made a brief return to competition, when he met Ireland's Mick O'Neill over five miles for £50 a-side at Ashton under Lyne on 11 November 1899. Over such short a distance, he was, of course, no match for the Irish four-mile champion of 1897 and 1898, who sprinted away on the last lap to win by 50 yards in 26:45.8, Len walking in.

Summing up, it had been a quiet year for Len – a disappointing one even – compared to the previous one. He had given a good account of himself in the Paris Marathon and over ten miles at Sittingbourne, but he had otherwise failed to live up to his own high expectations.

Rochdale, 16 September 1899: Harry Watkins (1) before his record-breaking one-hour run at Rochdale Athletic Ground, where he was paced by Len Hurst (2), Alex Haddow (3), Jack Walsh (4) and cyclist Harry Brown (5). The figure on the far right is believed to be Fred Bacon.

Several matches had been discussed but, as so often, they had failed to materialise. Then, in the second half of the year, when he seemed to be rediscovering his form, he fell ill, losing out on valuable weeks of training and prize money. The lot of the full-time professional athlete was always a precarious one as it relied entirely on him being fit and healthy. The fact that he had taken on the impossible task of racing Mick O'Neill over five miles shows that he was not in a great position financially. However, the hunger was still there. It would be interesting to see what the next century held for Sittingbourne's favourite son.

It was also around this time that Len contributed some notes on training to *Running Recollections and How to Train* by fellow professional

Alf Downer. Published the following year, the book retailed at 2s 6d and was endorsed by one well-known contemporary as something 'no athlete should be without'. It included 'short biographical sketches' of several prominent runners of the period. 'In offering a few hints on distance running,' Len modestly begins, 'I must crave the indulgence of my readers for the manner in which I may express myself, but as more of my time has been spent on the track than in the school, an apology is hardly necessary.' What follows are two pages of eye-opening details outlining the discipline and dedication he considers necessary to become a champion professional runner – an arcane blend of his own personal experience and wisdom gleaned over the years from his various acquaintances, advisors and trainers.

He suggests the following rigorous daily routine for aspiring distance runners:

Get up early (six o'clock in summer, seven in winter) and have a cold sponge down, then take a very brisk walk for an hour and a half before breakfast. After breakfast a further hour's walk followed by run at moderate pace for about half the distance of the race for which you are training. 'Remember never to overdo yourself, or pump yourself quite out,' he advises. After dinner an hour's rest in bed then the pattern of a walk followed by a run is repeated, this time with a sprint at the finish. This should be followed by a cold shower and rub down, paying careful attention to 'grooming'. Tea should be followed by a two-hour walk and then to bed at ten o'clock.

As for diet, he suggests for dinner beef, mutton or chicken, but limited amounts of vegetables and bread, and that the latter should be stale and crusty, and washed down with half-a-pint of good bitter ale. According to Alf Hurst, Len himself drank egg and sherry during races. His wife Ethel was his main source of support. She would rub him down after his morning run and have the raw eggs and steak ready.

It may be seen that Len did relatively little mileage for a marathon runner, only 40-50 miles of actual running per week. On the other hand, he also did a staggering amount of walking – some five-and-a-half-hours a day. This would, no doubt, have been done at a brisk pace, too. To fully understand this training methodology, it is important to remember the running shoes of that era did not afford good shock absorption and, therefore, a strong emphasis on walking would have enabled him to cover large distances on foot while minimising the risk of injury.

At a time when there was still little to be had in the way of nutritional and training literature, the advice he dispenses here would, to an aspiring runner, have been worth the price of the book alone. His mix of running, walking and massage would also stand up to modern scrutiny, although, of course, world-class marathon runners today eschew walking and run 100 miles a week or more. As a proponent of cold showers, Len would, no doubt, have approved of the ice baths, as popularised in recent times by the likes of Paula Radcliffe and Mo Farah.

It was another Olympic year. The upcoming Olympic Games in Paris would not have been on his mind as he prepared for the coming season,

Herwegh, Photo.]   [Edmonton.

LEN HURST.
*Champion of the World 20 Miles and Upwards, World's
Record Holder 16 and 17 Miles.*

This picture by Herwegh, Edmonton, is featured in Alf Downer's Running Recollections and How to Train.

but another event in Paris would have. For Len, success in the Paris-Conflans Marathon for professionals was crucial.

After a handful of low-key races in the spring of 1900, he tuned up for Paris in an unorthodox fashion. On 27 June he reopened his rivalry with Mick O'Neill in a ten-mile match for £100 before a large crowd at the Southport Sports Grounds. The match was witnessed by a large gathering, including, notably, George Tincler, Harry Watkins and Old Bill Lang, the former professional, who as the 'Crowcatcher' set world records in several running events in the 1860s and still held the world record for two miles. The race went pretty much by the book, a 'cat and mouse' affair, with the Irishman sprinting away on the last lap to win by 20 yards in 54:33.0.

Then, three days later, and only eight days before Paris, he ran another ten-mile match, this time against Fred Bacon, for £100 a-side at Southampton Football Ground before a disappointingly small crowd. Len, the newspaper reported, 'had been in training for twelve weeks … and … looked fit to race for his life, if need be.' The match followed a similar pattern to the one in Southport, with Bacon utilising his superior finishing speed to breast the tape a yard and a half to the good in 54:10.0.

While it would have come as no surprise to Len that he lost both matches, he would have been encouraged by the fact that he was twice able to run moderately fast times for ten miles within the space of only three days – a sure sign that he was in form for the marathon.

On Saturday, 7 July Len arrived in Paris in the company of his backer, J.W. Turner of Southport, his brother Joe and Mr Funk of Becconshall Hotel at Hescott Bank, near Preston, where he had been training on a miniature track. The next day, he was among the 124 peds to sign in for the annual 40-kilometre marathon race, which this year was to be run in the opposite direction – from Conflans to Paris – and conclude with two

Paris, 8 July 1900. Runners line up for the start of the Conflans-Paris Marathon. Len Hurst is in white shorts on the far right.

laps of the grass track at the Parc des Princes velodrome. The notoriously meticulous race organisers had mapped out a course, giving the exact distance to each checkpoint along the route in metres. This year, the runners were competing for a purse of F1,700, with F1,000 going to the winner – a good deal less than in previous years but still an attractive sum, nonetheless.

As the runners lined up for the start by the River Seine, Len cut a stylish figure in his blue running vest and white sateen drawers, his head covered with a knotted white handkerchief to ward off the sun, and his feet shod in hand-made running shoes with calf-leather uppers and India rubber soles. At 2pm Mr Paul Rousseau sent the runners on their way in brilliant sunlight. Camille Pottemain dé Laroque, a French nobleman who had finished sixth in the previous year's event, raced into an early lead but was eventually caught by a group of pursuers, which reached

Le passage du groupe de tête à Saint-Germain.

the checkpoint at Saint Germain (25.726km) in one hour 30 minutes. The contenders at this stage were Victor Bagré, André Suech, Pottemain, Robert Cheminel, Albert Charbonnel, and the easy striding figure of Len Hurst.

The race hotting up now, Bagré got away and, setting a blistering pace, established a lead of some 500 metres over the subsequent eight-kilometre stretch to Saint Cloud. However, the effort told on Bagre, who slowed noticeably in the closing stages, allowing Len, who had left the others well behind, to reduce the gap. Len finally snagged Bagré as they approached the Porte de Boulogne at around 37 kilometres. The leader, a bookbinder by trade, fell apart at the seams when his English rival sailed past him within sight of the Parc des Princes. After losing the lead, Bagré, it was reported, stopped and refused to continue but, urged on

Finishing scenes of the 1900 Conflans-Paris Marathon at Parc des Princes against the spectacular backdrop of the Eiffel Tower, built 11 years earlier.

by his friends, he eventually resumed and finished the race. Len, having judged his effort to perfection, finished full of running and notched up his second win in this event in a world-record time of 2:26:47.4. It was a truly ground-breaking performance, minutes faster than anything that had been accomplished previously on the road or track. His margin of victory spoke volumes; he finished over three minutes ahead of Bagré and five minutes ahead of the reigning champion, Charbonnel.

Afterwards, Charbonnel expressed his dissatisfaction with the result, claiming to have suffered a fall during the race, and that this had prevented him from winning. He issued a challenge to Len to run 20 miles, but although Len accepted, the match failed to materialise as Len had decided, at short notice, to compete in the Olympic Games.

The second Games of the modern Olympiade were held in conjunction with the Paris World's Fair in the summer of 1900. At the time, little or no reference was made to the fact that these were Olympic Games. They were variously described as either international contests or world championships. Most of the events in the track and field programme took place on a field at the Croix-Catelan Stadium, home to the Racing Club de Paris. The 1900 Games were arguably the most unconventional of the modern era. The swimming events, which included a bizarre obstacle race, were held in the River Seine, where strong currents swept the competitors to earth-shattering times. Motor racing made its one and only Olympic appearance at these games, and the clay-pigeon shooting competition is the only one in Olympic history to have featured actual live 'skeets'. Uniquely, the second Olympiade also showcased both amateur and professional athletics. In early May, *La Vie Au Grand Air* published a proposed programme, including details of entry fees and the values of prizes. There were to be divided into separate 'world championships' for amateurs and professionals. Ironically, some of the prizes on offer for the amateur events exceeded the value of those available to the professionals, the winner of the amateur 100 metres flat race, for instance, receiving a prize worth F150 more than the winner of the professional event. The amateur marathon race of 40 kilometres was won by France's Michel Theato in a shade under three hours. Theato would have been no match for Len, who was nearly 33 minutes quicker in the Conflans-Marathon 11 days previously. The British entrants had been culled from the previous year's London to Brighton race but were clearly not cut from the same rugged cloth as Len as they all dropped out during the first 10 kilometres.

A 'Six Hours' Championship of the World' for professionals was to be the culmination of the professional track and field events, held a fortnight after the amateur track and field programme had concluded. Carrying a purse of F2,550, with the winner to receive F1,500, this was the richest athletics event of the 1900 Olympic Games. The big question, though, was: was Len up to the task, just four weeks after a gruelling marathon?

Forty-three of the 51 athletes who had registered found their way to the Vélodrome de Vincennes on the morning of Sunday, 5 August 1900. The event, in keeping with the spirit of the games, had an international flavour. Entries included Len Hurst of England, Charles Immée and Paul Lambert of Belgium, Georg Buff of the Netherlands, William Lewis of Germany and the mysterious-sounding 'Ermolli' of Italy. The most prominent among the numerous French competitors were

Albert Charbonnel, Victor Bagré, Albert Chauvelot, Eugene Janvier, Eugene Neveu, Louis Orphee and Georges Fleury. When the starting signal was given at 11am, the men immediately sprang into action. The field was soon scattered around the 400-metre grass circuit as the race leaders set a brisk pace. Len chased the early leader, Chauvelot, through 10 kilometres in 38:45 and then went ahead to lead at the hour with 15.59km. After pulling the field through 20 kilometres in 1:20.05.2, Len gave way to Charbonnel, who drew away and at two hours (29.42km) led by 100 metres from Chauvelot, with Len another 100 metres behind. In the ensuing kilometres Len took closer order and, regaining the lead from Charbonnel, went through 35 kilometres in a world-record time of 2:25:31.4. At 40 kilometres Charbonnel was back in front, leading by a stride's length from Len in 2:48:04.8. The position was the same at the completion of three hours, Charbonnel having covered 42.504 kilometres. After the race entered its fourth hour, Len was able to shake off Charbonnel and build up a lead of three laps at 50 kilometres, accomplished in a world-record time of 3:36:45. Bagré, after making a cagey start, was now making inroads on the leaders and had relegated Charbonnel to third.

At the completion of four hours, Len had covered 54.136 kilometres, giving him his third world record of the race. The stage looked set for another great British triumph in Paris. But then disaster struck. His pace slowed to a crawl as he battled with what appeared to be the onset of stomach cramp. Was it cramp or simply exhaustion? Bagré seized his opportunity and moved into the lead with just over four and a half hours on the clock. Len, after taking an agonising 40 minutes to cover the next three kilometres, decided he could not continue and hobbled off to the dressing room after completing 61 kilometres in five hours and 15 minutes. Meanwhile, Bagré swept to victory by a margin of over a kilometre from Charbonnel with 72.545 kilometres, thus avenging his defeat in the Paris-Conflans Marathon. In retrospect, it can be said that Len had missed a golden opportunity to win the first, and only, professional long-distance championship in Olympic history.

Although the modern Olympic Games have traditionally been underpinned by the amateur code, they still had a profound impact on Len's professional running career. The inaugural Olympic-inspired Paris-Conflans Marathon had given him a golden opportunity to shine on the international stage. This, in turn, had given new impetus to his sporting career, propelling him toward the fringes of 19th-century superstardom.

The scene at the end of the 'Six Hours' Championship of the World' at Vincennes, with runners slugging what appears to be wine straight from the bottle.

Two months after his return from Paris, an offer by George Thurling of £25 induced Len to launch a bid to run 19½ miles in 1:51:54 – this being exactly George Crossland's world record for 20 miles. This match against 'time' took place at the North London Cycling and Athletic Grounds, Wood Green, on Saturday, 6 October 1900. The grounds, built in 1895 at a cost of £15,000, featured cycling and running tracks, the quarter-mile cinder running track being something of a novelty because it had banked turns. The conditions were not great. In fact, it was so windy, Len was initially hesitant and suggested a postponement until Monday, but his trainer, Jack Taylor, was having none of it and remarked, 'Get along and try it now. It will very likely be worse on Monday.' Given that a record looked out of the question in the circumstances, only 100 spectators were present when Len was sent on his way at 4pm. Paced by a couple of cyclists who rode out in front, and by fellow professionals Harry Watkins, Ted Shepherd and W. Matthews, who took it in turns to run a lap, he set a fast pace, completing five miles in 27:44.7, ten miles in 55:51.5, ten miles 1,270 yards in the hour, and 15 miles in 1:24:36.5. By starting more slowly than in his previous attempt, he was able to maintain a steady pace of less than six minutes a mile over the last five miles and, covering 19½ miles in 1:50:58, won the wager by 56 seconds. Then, without easing up, he kept going and finished with a fine sprint up the straight to complete 20 miles in a superb time of 1:53:42¼. At long last, the world professional record for this distance was indisputably his. It was even more remarkable an achievement considering the adverse weather conditions. The *Daily Mail* remarked that the strong wind 'certainly deterred him from making even faster time.' It was a pity Len did not run on after passing the finishing post, as he could have comfortably beaten George Crossland's outright world record of 20 miles 880 yards, set at Stamford Bridge in 1894.

This would have been a perfect end to the season had Len not agreed to run Billy Saward over 50 miles for £25 a-side at the Tee-To-Tum Grounds, Stamford Hill, on 17 November, only for the former Essex Beagle to forfeit his initial stake of £5. It left Len out of pocket. The rent for the track alone had set him back £2.

The previous year had brought a miraculous turnaround in Len's fortunes. What could the next year offer?

His campaign began in a low-key fashion with a series of handicap races between February and May, including a four-mile victory at White Hart Grounds in Tottenham Hale on 18 March in 21:50.0. On 8 April he defeated H. Jones at Lavender Hill for two miles for £5, probably his biggest payday during the early phase of the competitive season when the pickings were slim.

Of all the ironies, after a quiet pre-season he was forced to choose between two potentially lucrative opportunities, when of course he would much rather have availed himself of both. He had originally entered a six-day race at Royal Aquarium in early July, but then decided instead to defend his title in the concurrent Paris-Conflans Marathon.

With the race now in its fifth year, the marathon promoter L'Auto-Vélo had reverted to the original route after the previous year's change of route had been met with the vociferous opposition from the good citizens of Conflans. Len and his close rival Ted Shepherd were the only Brits in the starting field.

Arriving just on time for the start, Len quickly moved to the head of the 106-strong field that set off from Neuilly-sur-Seine in fine weather at 7am on 7 July. Victor Bagré started as the favourite but it soon became clear that he would not figure prominently. Albert Charbonnel, the winner of 1899, looked dangerous and launched an early attack on the outskirts of Ville-d'Avray (11,356km). On reaching the Versailles checkpoint at 16.8 kilometres in 1:00:58 he was 30 seconds ahead of Len, who, in turn, was 30 seconds ahead of Rigobert. Charbonnel kept up the fast pace so that he was out of sight of his nearest rivals when he passed the Saint-Germain checkpoint at 29.2 kilometres in 1:50:43. With just over ten kilometres to go, the Frenchman looked to have the race sewn up. Len was a clear second, but he was over three minutes in arrears of the flying Frenchman and the rest of the field were nowhere. However, Charbonnel was about to pay the price for his ambitious pace along the heavy route from Paris to Conflans.

Urged on by his brother Joe riding alongside, Len gradually began to peg back the deficit and by Croix de Noailles (34.7 kilometres) he had Charbonnel (2:15:00) in his sights again. So great was the crowd of cyclists accompanying Charbonnel that the signalman at the Acheres crossing had to stop the train in order to prevent an accident. When Len arrived at the crossing a minute or so later, he found the high level-crossing gate already blocking his path. He vaulted the gate, but his brother was less fortunate: he broke off the saddle of his bicycle in getting across and had an eventful ride to the finish. Despite having lost time and momentum negotiating the barrier, Len caught his flagging rival within sight of the finish and surged clear to win by around 100 yards in 2:34:52.4. For Len, the sweetness of this dramatic last-gasp victory was soured somewhat by a suspicion that he had been obstructed deliberately. Be that as it may, the French newspapers were as magnanimous as ever despite their disappointment over their man having lost such a commanding lead. G. De Lafreté writing in *La Presse* commented, 'Charbonnel ran a very good race and had the distance been a little shorter, I think he would beaten his redoubtable opponent.' Ultimately, then, it was Len's patience and pace judgement that had won the day and secured him his third win in this iconic race.

The result:

1	Len Hurst	England	2:34:52.4
2	Albert Charbonnel	France	2:35:19.2
3	Rigobert	France	2:44:20.4
4	Victor Bagre	France	2:45:13.2
5	Edmond Langlois	France	2:45:32
6	Paul Lafitte	France	2:50:51.4

Charbonnel subsequently challenged Len to a rematch, but was unable to come up with the stake money and nothing came of it. Much

Len is pictured here in hot pursuit of Charbonnel at Croix-de-Noailles, five kilometres from the finish.

like their British counterparts, the French professional runners were hardly able to live off their winnings. That year, *Le Petit Parisien* published a list of the prize money won by professional runners in France in 1901. Len was the top money-winner, with 1,000 francs from his single win in the Paris-Conflans Marathon, followed by Charbonnel, 985 francs; and

This competitor was – like Len Hurst – forced to negotiate a lowered level-crossing gate.

Len is pictured here with his brother after the race, Joe clutching his broken-off saddle.

Rigobert, 265 francs – 'It's not much,' the author wrote. The streets of Paris clearly weren't paved with gold. Far from it.

Six weeks after his triumph in Paris, Len took on Ted Shepherd in a match for the 'Twenty Miles Professional Championship' and a prize of £50 at Chatham and Brown's Ground in Grays in Essex. Shepherd,

36 years of age and 5ft 6in, boasted an impressive record of over 200 handicap wins since 1887. A father of six, he hailed from Higham near Gravesend and competed for the Essex Beagles as an amateur. At the same venue on 27 October of the previous year he had defeated the 1900 Olympian Billy Saward in a match over 15 miles in a good time of 1:29:29.2. The wealthy sporting enthusiast George Thurling added some spice to the occasion by offering an inducement, promising the winner £25 if he bettered the professional world record for 20 miles. The two rivals were sent on their way at 5.30pm in favourable weather, but the ground was reported to be 'rough' in places and not conducive to fast running. Around 700 spectators assembled round the quarter-mile track to watch the contest unfold. Len allowed Shepherd to set a leisurely pace for the first three miles before taking control. He was 20 yards ahead of his opponent at five miles (28:39) and over 300 yards ahead at ten miles, where split times of 57:44.5 and 58:50.5 were taken for himself and Shepherd respectively. After being lapped, Shepherd gave up at 12½ miles. Len had covered 13¼ miles in 1:16:36¾ when Shepherd gave him his consent to stop should he wish to do so. With the pace having been too slow for any chance of a new record, Len did no more than he needed to.

A match against the American Bob Hallen was the next to be arranged, but before then Len and his brother Joe ran an unusual 20-mile match against time for a purse of gold subscribed by some local sporting gentlemen at the Eureka Athletic Ground in Ponders End. The brothers, running simultaneously, had undertaken to jointly cover 20 miles in

The Tee-To-Tum Grounds in Stamford Hill.

less than one hour. Despite the inclement weather, they accomplished the task with two minutes and 45 seconds to spare, Len making an impressive contribution of ten miles 930 yards and his 44-year-old sibling accounting for the remainder.

Monday, 23 September was the day of reckoning – a race described by *The Times* as 'the most important pedestrian match seen in London for some years'. The contest was for the 'Twenty Five Miles Championship of the World' with stakes of £25 a-side. The venue chosen was the Tee-To-Tum Grounds in Stamford Hill, home to a fine cinder track measuring five laps to the mile. His opponent, Bob Hallen, was, judging by the hype at least, a formidable one. A fifth-placer in the 1899 Boston Marathon as a 19-year-old, the young New Yorker arrived in London as the '20 and 25 Miles Champion of America'. The much-awaited match attracted a crowd of some 4,000 to 5,000 spectators, a number which, it was reported, 'had not been seen at a professional footrace in London since Walter George raced against William Cummings at Lillie Bridge.' Len started as the 6-to-4 favourite, having trained without coaching assistance at Edmonton. The match got off to a pedestrian start at around 3.15pm, Hallen cutting out the pace for the first few laps before surging into a lead of 25 yards, which Len quickly nullified. After another lap the American broke away again and this time got 80 yards in front before Len set about pegging him back again. Was he playing cat and mouse with the young American? It appears so. After four miles, Len got serious and left Hallen standing, gaining 34 seconds within the space of the next mile. Although completely outclassed, the American persevered but eventually gave up after being lapped three times and consented to Len stopping. At this juncture the promoter stepped in and offered Len a gold medal if he could beat the 21-mile record of 2:06:21 held by George Dunning. However, the crowd, perhaps thinking the race was over, invaded the track and caused an obstruction, forcing Len to give up opposite the dressing room 30 yards shy of 13 miles in 1:17:45. Nevertheless, 'it was,' wrote the *North Middlesex Standard*, 'a good race, and the winner was immensely popular.'

Having failed to get the record in his race against Hallen, Len returned to the Tee-To-Tum Grounds a week later for an attempt to beat William

Howitt's age-old 15-mile record for an undisclosed sum. However, wet and windy weather conspired to make this an near-impossible task. Despite the best efforts of a cyclist and his brother Joe, and the vociferous support of 1,000 spectators, he was forced to retire after having covered ten miles in 56:09.5.

On Saturday, 16 November Len was back at the Tee-To-Tum Grounds to make an assault on George Mason's professional world records for 21 to 25 miles. 'A well-known sportsman,' wrote the *Nottingham Evening Post*, 'had agreed to back Time, and stake £20 to £30', £50 in all. To win the wager Len had to beat the following times: 21 miles 2:08:35; 22 miles, 2:15:17; 23 miles, 2:23:33; 24 miles, 2:30:04; and 25 miles, 2:36:34. Without the added spur of competition, the odds of him succeeding were set at 3 to 2 against. The sunny and windless conditions would have been ideal had it not been bitterly cold; in fact, the track was frost-bound. Some of the old-timers present shook their heads when discussing the effect the hard surface was likely to have on the feet of a runner wearing spikes. With pacing being provided by cyclist Charlie Munro and fellow pedestrian George Crossland, Len set off at a judicious pace, covering five miles in 29:30.5 and ten miles in 59:36.5. Having made ten miles 165 yards in the first hour, he had three minutes in hand. After that, however, it all went wrong. As the old timers had predicted, the combination of hard ground and spikes wreaked blistering havoc on his feet, and he gave up in agony after covering 14¾ miles in 1:29:27¾.

That was it for the 1901 season. Even though he hadn't succeeded in setting any records, it had been a very successful year capped by two championship titles and a memorable triumph in the Paris Marathon. That winter, Len finally called time on his career as a brickmaker. The truth of the matter was that the days of the brickmaker were numbered as a consequence of technological progress; the future lay in mechanised brickmaking, not manual labour. Instead, Len and Ethel jointly opened a greengrocer's shop in Hertford Road, Edmonton. This first step towards independence not only gave the family a steady income, but it also enabled Len to train when it suited him.

The year 1902 began with a trip to America, the land of opportunity. Len and his brother Joe had signed up for the 'Six Days' Championship of the World' at New York's Madison Square Garden. The contest, the latest venture of American sporting supremos Powers and Kennedy, was a six-day go-as-you-please foot race, there being teams of two instead of individual competition. Len Hurst, wrote Tommy Hall, the English racing cyclist who recruited him and his brother, 'is the best man in England today. He holds the world's record for 24 hours, 160 miles, beating Charlie Rowell's famous run made in Madison Square Garden on November 1 1880, by more than ten miles.' This figure of 160 miles in 24 hours was, of course, a pure fabrication, but it was regurgitated by all the leading US newspapers and ensured that the Hurst brothers were odds-on favourites to win. After receiving a rousing send-off from Waterloo Station, the brothers sailed from Southampton on 18 January aboard the American Line steamer *St. Paul* and disembarked at Ellis Island, New York, exactly seven days later. The *New York Times* reported that 'the brothers are entered in the six-day, go-as-you-please race, which will begin in Madison Square Garden on Feb. 10th, and are backed by a syndicate of Englishmen, headed by Charley Mitchell (a former Champion of England prize fighter [sic]). They arrived in splendid condition and will finish their training at Sheepshead Bay with several other pedestrians who are getting into shape there for the event.'

The contest was the first of its kind for many years, six-day races having last flourished in the USA during the 1880s. The rules decreed that competitors could walk or run but that no man could remain on the track for more than 12 hours out of 24. With an advertised $5,000 in prize money and prizes ranging in value from $1,500 (£300) for the winners to $125 for the tenth-placed team, the contest attracted the interest of no fewer than 43 teams from all corners of the globe, including several well-known old-timers. Being favourites, the Hurst brothers wore bib numbers '1' and '2'.

The track was surfaced with tan bark, loam and sawdust, being ten laps to the mile and 12 feet wide. Tents had been set up around the circumference of the track for the competitors. The management had also arranged for physicians to be in attendance round the clock to look after the well-being of the competitors.

The word 'go' was given at 12.20am on 10 February by champion heavyweight boxer James Jeffries before a crowd some 6,000 spectators. The brothers got off to a good start, Len running first, and they were lying in fifth place after nine hours with 66 miles 1,741 yards. Then, however, they slipped down the order when they were forced to retire for three hours due to both men experiencing knee trouble.

Early in the morning of day two, Joe had the misfortune to turn his ankle. Len, at the time, was in his tent being doctored for a swollen knee so Joe bravely remained on the track until his brother was dressed and ready to go. The latter stayed on the track for about ten hours until Joe finally reappeared. Despite the injury, Joe gained several laps shortly before midnight, but the mishap had cost them their place in the top ten. At the end of day two, they were down in 19th place with 223.6 miles. Day three only saw them move up a few places. However, the brothers remained upbeat and, 'running like demons' in the early hours of day four, overcame their soreness to make up mile after mile, moving up into ninth after 88 hours with 428 miles and then improving to seventh after 95 hours with 461 miles 34 yards. Their efforts had been the highlight of an otherwise dull fourth day, although there was some drama on the sidelines when Peter Hegelman of the leading team, crazed by a combination of stimulants, sleep deprivation and fatigue, swore one of his attendants was poisoning him and smashed a bottle over his head before being dragged away and sedated with opiates. When he awoke three hours later, he had no recollection of his demented fit and asked his trainer why his head was bandaged.

There were still 16 teams in the race at this stage, and the backers of the English duo were hopeful they would continue to move up the order, but at 10pm Len had to stop, his nose bleeding, and Joe was only able to limp round, with the result that they fell back from seventh to ninth.

The brothers' overambitious efforts on the fourth day had the effect of reducing them to physical wrecks, and on day five they slumped to 14th place after 120 hours with a score of 494.3 miles. The *Rochester New York Democrat Chronicle* reported that 'Len Hurst, of the English team, is scarcely able to walk about the track.' Their problems were compounded when one of their trainers gave them the wrong food and drink, and Joe became violently ill when it was his turn to take to the track, at one point collapsing. Being in no fit state to continue, they retired at about 4am on the last day after covering an undisclosed distance (about 500 miles).

A wealthy spectator, Lord Algernon Lennox, was so touched by the gallant efforts of the pair that he made them a handsome monetary gift, which was unexpected and received with humble gratitude.

The $1,500 first prize went to the Irish-American pairing of Peter Hegelman and Patrick Cavanaugh, who jointly amassed 770.4 miles. The winning team, the *Chicago Sunday Tribune* revealed, had spent $200 on food and training. In six days they had consumed two pounds of steak, 20 dozen eggs, one pound of coffee, five pounds of malted milk, half a pound of tea, half a dozen bottles of ale, a dozen stalks of celery, four cans of peas, and 20 gallons of water.

A day after the race had concluded, it was reported that after enjoying Turkish baths and plenty of sleep the competitors appeared at the Putnam

House bar in New York, where they spent the afternoon chatting and smoking cigars.

The brothers sailed back to England on 20 February. That day, it was announced that a 25-mile sweepstake had been arranged to be run in Philadelphia in April and that Len would be competing. This race did not, however, materialise. In fact, Len would never set foot on US soil again.

Four weeks after his return to England, Len was back in action at the Tee-To-Tum Grounds on Saturday, 28 March. With sizeable money prizes on offer for the first three places, the field was of course a strong one. Although Len was still feeling the after-effects of his exertions in America, he did well to finish second in 57 minutes, 300 yards behind Fred Bacon (56:10.6) and 350 yards ahead of Tom Collins of Barking.

It had been over a year since he last raced against Fred Bacon, who had been conspicuous by his absence from UK competition the previous year. Rumours had it that he had spent the year touring Europe and winning races in places as far afield as Paris, Algiers and Berlin. However, the pair were united by mutual interests and a close friendship, which they appear to have rekindled when they met at the Tee-To-Tum Grounds.

Following his defeat in the ten miles at Stamford Hill, Len journeyed north to Scotland in early May for a rematch against Bacon over the same distance at the Alloa Recreation Grounds, where they were racing for a purse given by H. F. Dyer of the Red Lion Hotel, Portland Street, London. One may well ask why such a match should be decided in

Scotland. The answer is that Bacon was at the time employed as a trainer at the Edinburgh Powderhall Ground and was based in Alloa, where he had evidently hit a fine vein of form. Prior to his convincing victory in the ten-mile championship at Stamford Hill, he had set a Scottish all-comers' ten-mile record of 52:51.4 at Alloa on 1 February. A bumper crowd, a good track and fine weather all made for excellent racing. As was typical of their encounters, Bacon and Hurst kept close together throughout, each taking turns at leading. Again, as usual, a decent pace was set. Bacon was said to be 'the prettier runner of the two', while Len's style was described as 'exceedingly ungainly and not by any means prepossessing'. Be that as it may, there was nothing in it until the home straight, where Bacon produced his trademark grandstand finish to win by a dozen yards in 54:24.0 to 54:26.5.

The following month Len again met Bacon in a 15-mile match at the Tee-To-Tum Grounds £25 a-side, plus half net gate receipts and the Championship of the World. Unfortunately for Bacon, he had to give up half-way through the race due to a cold and therefore gifted Len an easy win, the latter stopping at $8^1/_5$ miles in 47:24.

Next up for Len was his annual excursion to Paris, where he was chasing a fourth win in the marathon race on Sunday, 6 July 1902. That year prize money was available for the first 15 finishers, starting with 1,000 francs for the winner, F300 for second, F200 for third, down to F20 for 15th. There was also a special prize of 50 francs for the fastest last kilometre among the first 20 finishers. The distance was still 40 kilometres, but the course had been changed to allow the race to start at Conflans and finish with a kilometre on the dirt track at the Buffalo Velodrome. Usually the race had been run early in the morning well before the sun had reached its mid-day apex, but on this occasion, in order to accommodate the spectators at the Buffalo Velodrome, the promoters had decided to start the race at 1pm. To make matters worse, for the first time since the event's inception the runners were confronted with heatwave conditions. Len and Charlie Hart were the only Britons in the field of 122 runners that set off from Conflans in blazing sunshine. Under these extreme conditions, the runners were more dependent than usual on support. As an outsider, however, Len could not expect any great help. The French elite runners therefore had a clear advantage. He was up among the leaders until Saint Germain (8 km), but then lost ground on the next part of the route to Versailles (21.2 km) where the young Corsican Felix Vianzoni was first with one hour 23 minutes, followed a minute later by Albert Charbonnel, and then Len and Gustave Thomas, both 50 metres behind Charbonnel.

A scene from the early stages of the 1902 Conflans-Paris Marathon: Len Hurst (X), Albert Charbonnel (2), Eugène Neveu (125) and Gustave Thomas (17).

Charbonnel disposed Vianzoni of the lead soon after leaving Versailles and had built a good lead by Suresnes checkpoint (32.98 kilometres), which he passed in 2:15:08, well before Len (2:17:43) and Vianzoni (2:19:30). Maintaining a steady pace, Charbonnel arrived at the Buffalo Velodrome with a comfortable lead and was cheered home enthusiastically by his many supporters. He had nearly finished his last kilometre on the track when a cheer went up to announce the arrival of the next runner. It was Len. However, he was clearly done for and just 50 yards ahead of a fast-closing Gustave Thomas. Badly dehydrated, Len gave no answer when Thomas blew past him with a lap to go to take second place and the prize for the fastest last kilometre. Nevertheless, by finishing third, Len had maintained an impressive record of making the top three in every Paris-Conflans race since its inception. The winning time was the slowest in the history of the event, giving some idea of how tough the race had been. Only three men managed to beat three hours and only 50 completed the distance. Olympic Champion Michel Théato, who had been expected to provide a serious challenge, did not figure prominently and was over 26 minutes behind the winner in ninth place. Len's performance was all the more remarkable when one considers that he ran without the aid of a cyclist until the final stages of the race, when three French cyclists got hold of lemons and sponges to keep him going. All the other competitors were reportedly being freshened

Arrivée du vainqueur : Charbonnel (Français).   Thomas (Français).   Hurst (Anglais).

Les trois premiers de la course pédestre dite de Marathon. — Phot. Lefebvre.

up at every moment with new-fangled spray pumps containing ammonia, alcohol and camphor.

Afterwards, a rather dejected Len said, 'Soon after the start I lost sight of my pacemaker, nobody looked after me, and had but a lemon given me. This is my last race of this sort. 'Tis too far for me on the road.'

The result:

1	Albert Charbonnel	France	2:52:05
2	Gustave Thomas	France	2:55:55
3	Len Hurst	England	2:56:40
4	Felix Vianzoni	France	3:01:35
5	Eugène Neveu	France	3:03:55
6	Henri Prévot	France	3:12:02

It was a testament to Len's prodigious recuperative powers that only one week after the gruelling Conflans-Paris race he was able to take part in the

'European Professional Championships' at the Buffalo Velodrome. The championships, a prototype of the European Athletics Championships inaugurated in 1934, were organised by the Club Athlétique Parisien and consisted of a small selection of events including handicap races. The showpiece event was the 10,000 metres, with 20 entries including Gustave Thomas, Albert Charbonnel and Fred Bacon. As it was obvious to assume that the marathon runners would still be tired from their exertions a week before, Bacon ensured a fast pace from the start. Within just two laps of the 250-metre track he had shaken off all his opponents, except a sprightly-looking Gustave Thomas. In the end, though, Bacon left it to a sprint finish and won by ten metres from Thomas in 34:26.5 and by 100 metres from Len, who, after a steady start, had worked his way up to third place. The next day Len competed in the 1,500 metres, an unusually short distance for him, and surprisingly came second behind Gustave Thomas in 4:31.5.

On 20 July Len returned to Buffalo to take part in an international one-hour team race that had been billed as a 'battle royale' between the best professionals from England and France. The winners were to receive 1,000 francs (£16) and 500 francs (£8) would go to the losers. Once again he had his arch rivals Bacon, Thomas and Charbonnel to deal with. With an additional week to recover from the rigours of the marathon, however, he was almost his old self again. Taking the lead at the half-way mark, he completed 10,000 metres in 34:43.8, with only Charbonnel for company. With Charbonnel still clipping at his heels as the hour approached, Len

The line-up for the international one-hour race at Buffalo: (from left to right) Gustave Thomas, Len Hurst, Albert Charbonnel and Fred Bacon.

launched a long sprint and won by five metres from Charbonnel with a distance of 16,870 metres (ten miles 858 yards). With Bacon at 16,665 metres, the two Brits easily won the team competition.

After the close finish to the hour's race at Buffalo, a rematch was quickly arranged. This so-called 'revenge match' was decided the following week before a crowd of nearly 4,000 spectators. Prior to the rematch, British cyclist Tom Linton had to abandon an attempt to beat the paced one-hour cycling record due to the strong wind. The windy conditions also ruled out a record in the one-hour running match, but once again Len prevailed, winning by 50 metres from Fred Bacon with a distance of 16,700 metres.

Two great rivals pose together for the camera at Buffalo: Len Hurst and Fred Bacon.

Len wrapped up the 1902 season with a ten-mile handicap on Boxing Day at the Old Bow Grounds in London. The venue, home to a six-and-a-half-lap grass track, was a local mecca of pedestrianism thanks to the tireless efforts of its owner, Tom Jackson, who held weekly meetings here until about 1910. The race attracted the interests of a number of well-known athletes, including Bob Hallen, Abe Crudgington, Arthur

Flaunty, Tom Jackson, William Vinall, Jack Mansfield, Tom Dance, George Connor, John Punter and Jack Regan. The first prize was, after all, a handsome gold and silver champion belt supposedly crafted by Goldsmiths & Silversmiths Co. The race was framed as a handicap and Len was at scratch and giving away very big leads to his rivals. The bookmakers were so confident that he would fail they were offering odds of 10 to 1 against him winning. However, these were just numbers to Len. He was determined to get his hands on the champion belt. Running like a demon, he caught one opponent after another. On the penultimate lap he finally caught up with the leading runner Tom Jackson and then uncorked a powerful finish that carried him to victory by 20 yards. The champion belt was a thing of beauty and a prize he would cherish for the rest of his days.

During his long career Len had achieved much, but by no means everything. He had won professional world championships at 15, 20 and 25 miles. He had won the iconic Paris Marathon – the world's oldest city marathon – no fewer than three times. He had set professional world records at every distance from 13 to 20 miles. He had also set world records for 35 kilometres, 50 kilometres and four hours. He had beaten all the best professional runners of his era at least once, and had earned the right to be regarded as the world's greatest marathon runner of his day. But there was a blemish: he still needed a world record for 25 miles. Despite several attempts, he had not yet managed to beat either the amateur record or the professional record. In the 1900 Conflans-Paris

This picture of Len Hurst from around 1903 shows him wearing the silver champion belt gained at Bow on Boxing Day 1902.

Marathon he had covered 40 kilometres – just 200 metres shy of 25 miles – in 2:26:48. In order to claim his long overdue place of honour in the record books, he also needed Lady Luck on his side for once.

Len opened his 1903 account by accepting the challenge of Charlie Hart to run for 15 hours and stakes of £50 a-side at the Tee-To-tum Grounds on 23 March. The 36-year-old Clapham professional had gained a measure of celebrity the month before by completing 2,000 miles in 31 consecutive days at St John's Hill Baths, Clapham, and he was brimming with confidence.

As was the custom, both protagonists went into special training for the match. Hart, the *Weekly Guardian* wrote, had been 'causing much interest in the neighbourhood of Carshalton', while Len, it was reported, was evoking similar attention on the roads in and around Epping Forest. Both protagonists would have been mortified to read that a military band had been engaged in order to 'relieve the monotony' and that the club had thrown open their billiard saloons to the public on this day in order that 'a few interesting hours may be spent away from the track'. They were dispatched shortly after seven o'clock in the morning. Len got off to a flying start, covering 9.6 miles in the first hour, 18.4 miles in two hours and 26.0 miles in three hours. He was leading Hart by eight laps after three hours but had to leave the track twice during the next two hours and, as a result, lost his lead. In the afternoon, however, he rallied to re-take the lead, completing 50 miles in 6:53:15. But Hart refused to let up and twice regained the lead, in the tenth hour and again in the 14th hour.

Charlie Hart gave Len a run for his money in a 15-hour match at the Tee-To-Tum Grounds in 1903.

With one hour to go, Hart was three laps ahead and on his way to victory. However, Hart's ankles were really troubling him and, despite being very exhausted, Len seized the opportunity to fight back and win by five laps with 89.6 miles (144 kilometres). The Clapham man had given him a good run for his money and pushed him to the limit. After such a close race, Hart was of course keen on a rematch and immediately threw out a challenge, but Len had no desire to tackle such a long distance again any time soon; as far as he was concerned, he had proved all there was to prove in the 15-hour race. Fortunately for Hart, an opportunity for vengeance was about to present itself.

For some inexplicable reason long-distance walking races on the road became phenomenally popular in 1903. In Len's neck of the woods the most prestigious road race had for many years been the London to Brighton. The classic route was a 52¼ mile stretch of south London, Surrey and Sussex roads from the Westminster Bridge to the Brighton Aquarium via Croydon, Purley, Horley, Crawley, Bolney, Hickstead,

Pyecomb, Patcham and Preston. It had been popular among pedestrians since this first go-as-you-please match in 1837, when John Townshend defeated John Berry after an epic battle in eight hours 35 minutes. After that, the Brighton road was often the scene of matches and record attempts. The walking record of 8:56:44 had been set by Teddy Knott, an amateur, in 1897. The running record of 6:58:18 had also been set by an amateur – Fred Randall, of Finchley Harriers, in 1899. The next pivotal event was the Stock Exchange Walk of 1903, when about 100 members of the London Stock Exchange held their first walking race to Brighton. Some of the participants even wore suits and top hats and the race caused quite a sensation, with crowds turning out in force to watch the spectacle. The great success of this event encouraged *The Evening News* of London to promote a go-as-you-please race for professionals on 20 June 1903. The prize money, 50 guineas for the winner, ten guineas for second and five guineas for third, down to £1 for each of the next 15, was supplemented by various gifts. The first runner to reach Brighton wearing a Palatine Revolving Heel pad would receive £5 from the manufacturer. The first athlete who passed Messrs. Tudor and Co. shop in London Road, Croydon, would be given a York Ham. The Wawkphar Co, owners of the 'British and Indian Military Strengthening Foot Powder', offered £5 and a six dozen case to the winner, provided the powder had been used during the race, and 'New Skin' – a liquid preparation to stop blisters and soreness – promised £5 to the first competitor who reached the finish wearing 'New Skin' on his feet.

Len prepared for the race by doing long endurance-building runs on the leafy roads around Epping. Twelve days before the big race he tuned up by running ten miles from Brewer's Hotel to Cheshunt and back on the Hertford Road in four minutes under the hour for an undisclosed sum.

His main threats were thought to be Charlie Hart, eager to avenge his recent defeat (he had reportedly covered the course in seven hours 33 minutes in a trial run); Billy Saward, who had finished second in the 1899 amateur race in 7:17:50; and Abe Crudgington, winner of the 40-mile London to Southend race just 19 days earlier.

It was exactly 5am when the runners, 91 in number, were sent on their way in the pouring rain. They were a motley body of casual and serious 'peds'; some with training and others with no known prior form; including an octogenarian of 85. Several of the competitors had advertisements for athletic warehouses such as Gammages on their jerseys. This was the dawn of corporate sponsorship and product endorsement and the 1903 London to Brighton race for professionals was, it is believed, something of a litmus test. Len was the favourite and had backed himself to win all the prizes. He was described by *The Evening News* as a young man of medium height (he stood 5ft 9in and weighed 10st 4lb) with a very slight moustache, wearing a blue jersey and white breeches. Amid the rush of the competitors was one in a morning suit, another carrying a malacca cane and a third leisurely smoking a cigarette.

Various refreshments were available en route: Hot Horlick's Malted Milk could be drunk at six points along the course, Bovril at a range of public houses along the course, and Oxo could be obtained from an accompanying motor car. Some exotic concoctions were available from this vehicle – Oxo and soda, and Oxo and champagne, as well as eau de Cologne 'to bathe parched lips and face'.

Len was attended to by his brother Joe, who rode alongside on a bicycle, while a motor car ferrying the judges and timekeepers also watched over the proceedings.

Len adopted his favourite racing tactic, which was to let them go, to wait, and let them come back to him. He ran his own race for the first 13 miles, and then moved up to join the leaders, who reached Mutton's Hotel at Redhill (20¾ miles) in 2:11:30. Himself and Vinall then broke away from Crudgington to reach the Chequers Hotel at Horley (24¼ miles) in 2:35:35 and Povey Cross (26 miles) in around two hours 50 minutes. Maintaining a relentless space, he finally managed to shake off the diminutive Eastbourne runner on the stretch to Crawley. By the time he passed the George Hotel at Crawley (29¼ miles in 3:12:10), he was already one-and-a-half minutes ahead of Vinall, who paid the price for his overexuberance in the second half of the race and slumped to 12th place. The nine-mile stretch to Bolney (38 miles 398y in 4:25:30) saw Len extend his lead to three miles. By Hickstead he was nearly four miles ahead. The race already decided, he allowed himself to take occasional walking breaks on the final run-in to Brighton, where the *Sporting Life* correspondent observed in his rolling gait a tell-tale sign of excessive stimulant use. The use of stimulants such as strychnine was at the time

This real-photo postcard shows Len Hurst en route to winning the 1903 London to Brighton race. The accompanying cyclist on the right of picture is his brother Joe.

LEN HURST, Winner of "Go-as-you-please" Race, London to Brighton, June 20, 1903, in the record time of 6 hrs. 34 mins. 50 sec.

tolerated and commonplace, even among amateurs, but the line between stimulation and intoxication was a thin one easily crossed. No doubt the stimulants had been liberally administered by Joe, who was not exactly a medical professional. After passing Preston Park at Brighton (50½ miles in 6:16:12), he was also slowed by heavy traffic and people holding billboards. However, the sight of the aquarium half a mile in the distance and the large crowds by the roadside brought him back to life and he finished in style amid an uproar of cheers and motor horns. He had taken 6:34:50 and beaten the record by over 23 minutes. He was so little distressed by his efforts that shrewdly he sat down and wrote with a steady hand that thanks to 'New Skin' he had finished the race with his feet in perfect condition. H.S. Bell of New Barnet, a 'dark horse', finished second in 7:13:07 and Charlie Hart, after a slow start, arrived third, but well beaten, in 7:21:58. About 40 to 50 finished the race, although well spread out. Most of the competitors finished the course within the 15-hour time limit. The liquid refreshment along the course had served the competitors well. The Oxo vehicle had, it was announced, given out 300 flasks of Oxo, 107 glasses of Oxo and champagne, 221 cups of plain Oxo, and a quart of eau de Cologne.

In addition to the prize money he won and the bonus awarded by New Skin, Len received a fee for granting the famous Gamage's department store in Holborn the right to use his name in an ad which read, 'The BRIGHTON 'GO-AS-YOU-PLEASE' Won by LEN HURST in RECORD TIME in GAMAGE'S SHOES and CLOTHING. Other aspirants to fame please note – If you are walking or running please give us a call.' His name was also used to endorse an embrocation product in an advert worded thus: 'It was is no doubt due to Karmelite Embrocation that I used to-day that I was able to beat the record by twenty-six minutes, and I felt wonderfully fresh at the finish. I shall use it regularly in future.' It is astonishing to think that he was doing all of this over 80 years before the first amateur was able to legally procure endorsement contracts and commercial sponsorship, but what today is considered normal was vilified by the guardians of the amateur ideal at the time.

The impact Len had after his London-Brighton triumph can be gauged by the reports that he received a 'royal reception' on his return to Edmonton and that his feat, according to the *Middlesex Gazette* at least, was 'the sole topic, perhaps, locally'. It also gave the amateur camp food for thought. Fred Randall's course record had at the time been considered something of a quantum leap: no one before him had managed to complete the 52¼-mile course in under eight hours, let alone in under seven. Len, of course, had a reputation that preceded him, but he had hardly been expected to break the record by such a margin. This victory also had a special significance for Len in that he was finally able to prove his road-running ability in his home country: his greatest road races to date had all been abroad.

After two exhausting long-distance races within the space of eight weeks, Len decided to pass up the chance to run in the Paris Marathon again. The reason reported was 'indisposition' (malaise), but it is worth remembering that, after the debacle of the previous year, he had expressed his intention not to compete there anymore. The upside of that was of course that he had all the time he needed to recover from his exertions and prepare for his next venture, which was an attempt on the professional 25-mile record at the Preston Park Ground in Brighton on Thursday, 27 August 1903. His sights were now firmly set on breaking the 2:36:34 credited to George Mason in a 50-mile race at Lillie Bridge on 14 March 1881. Judging by the form, he knew he had a realistic chance at breaking the outright world record of 2:33:44 set by amateur George Dunning on 26 December of the same year.

As in his previous solo runs against the clock, he would have the help of pacemakers. The track was in good condition and known for fast times: the amateur champion Alfred Shrubb had set an amateur four-mile world record of 19:31.6 a year earlier. Built in 1877, the velodrome was the oldest in Great Britain and the second oldest in the world, measuring 633 yards per lap.

Tom Olliver helped pace Len Hurst to a 25-mile world record.

After the 'free show' of the London to Brighton race there were only 500 paying spectators present at the start at half past four, 'proof,' wrote the *Kentish Advertiser*, 'of the lessened interest in professional pedestrianism'. This may be so, but the promoters do not seem to have gone to particularly great lengths to publicise the record attempt.

To ensure authenticity, Mr J.T. Hulls had been appointed by the *Sporting Life* as the timekeeper and referee. Len was to be paced by his brother Joe, Tom Olliver of Brighton and a lesser-known cyclist. However, the conditions were good; there was almost no wind at all. As if a world-record attempt was enough of an attraction in itself, 'the proceedings,' a local newspaper reported, were to be 'enlivened by music performed by the Brighton Artisans' Band.'

Len, who was first paced by his brother and then by Tom Olliver, a rising star of distance running, began cautiously and made steady progress. Sticking closely to a schedule of six minutes per mile, Len covered the first ten miles in 59:37. At this point in the run he was still two minutes 15 seconds slower than George Mason when he set the record. In fact, he didn't get inside Mason's figures for the first time until 20 miles had been completed. For the first 20 miles of the journey, Olliver had shouldered most of the pace-making work and had taken only a few breaks in between. The timekeeper called out 'two hours one minute and 12 seconds'. He was now seven seconds ahead of Mason and on course for a brilliant time, but well outside Dunning's 20-mile split of 1:59:21. Looking remarkably fit, Len maintained his steady rhythm and covered the next three miles in 6:25, 6:28 and 6:35. In comparison, Dunning had allowed himself over seven minutes per mile in this phase of his record run. For the first time, the elusive amateur record was within reach, provided he could run the last two miles in about six and a half minutes apiece. The strain was written on his face. After a hard-fought penultimate mile, Len summoned his last reserves and gave it everything on the last lap as the crowd did their best to urge him on. After a short but tense wait, Mr Hulls announced that Len had completed the distance in 'two hours thirty-three minutes and forty ... two seconds'. Just imagine, he had finally done it. He had not only eclipsed the professional world record but also, by the finest of margins, the amateur record, too. It had been a triumph of sound pace judgement and steely nerve. In that moment Len would have felt no exhaustion, but rather that serene sense of elation at having finally achieved a lifetime goal.

In addition to breaking the 25-mile record, he had rewritten the record books by setting new world records at every intermediate distance between 21 and 25 miles: records that would be documented with meticulous attention to detail in sporting almanacs such as the *Sporting Chronicle Annual*.

After his record run in Brighton nobody would have resented Len taking a break. However, he had other ideas. Only two days later, at

Eley's Athletic Ground in Ponder's End, he confounded the bookmakers by winning a four-mile race against a rival professional (W. Matthews) competing under the alias 'A. Aldridge' for a purse of gold given by a local 'sporting gentleman'. It was a bad joke on the part of Matthews to compete under such a pseudonym, because the like-named individual was a top-class amateur and could, as a result, have come under investigation by the ever-watchful Amateur Athletic Association.

After a highly profitable summer season Len was financially in a position to fulfil a long-held ambition: to open his own pub and make his mark as an innkeeper, thus following in the footsteps of countless other well-known athletes at the end of their sporting careers. Although there was a pub on virtually every corner in those days, sporting celebrities had a head start over their licensed victualling rivals. Being a novice to the pub business, Len applied for and received a limited six-day licence to sell beer. Licences for public houses – which were also eligible to sell spirits – were subject to approval by magistrates and difficult to obtain, while licences for beer houses were more readily available. Len's first establishment was the Turner's Arms in Devonshire Street in the east London district of Mile End.

Despite the distractions of becoming a pub landlord, Len still had no intention of hanging up his racing shoes yet, and later that year he accepted an invite from Paris to take part in a 50-mile go-as-you-please race for professionals. Note, 50 miles and not 50 kilometres. Although metric distances were the norm in mainland Europe, distances based on the Imperial system of measurement still enjoyed a measure of popularity in the non-Anglophone countries where athletics was an emerging sport modelled on the British prototype.

His preparations may not have been as extensive as usual, but his form was still there. In late September he easily defeated a two-man relay team in a six-mile race at Ponder's End.

The so-called 'Les 50 Milles a Buffalo' was held at Buffalo Velodrome on 15 November. Len was the only foreigner to be invited, so, as claimed, the race had an international, if weak, flavour. He was competing against six well-known French runners in Gustave Thomas, Henri Prévot, Albert Charbonnel, Eduard Cibot, Georges Fleury and Victor Bagré. The French participants had a relatively modest goal in Fleury's national record of 8:42:12, but they also, no doubt, had more ambitious goals in mind, such as the outdoor world record of 6:18:26.2 and the indoor world record of 5:55:04.5 held by English runners Jimmy Fowler-Dixon and George Cartwright respectively. Each runner had been allowed two pacemakers, but Len was content with one after recruiting his compatriot Tommy Hall, a well-known professional rider. He was also looked after by Joe Smith, an old friend and masseur at Alma Gymnasium in London.

The ground conditions were good – a firm and well-trodden 250-metre grass track marked by wooden posts on the infield of the steeply banked cycle track. The weather was fine when the competition got underway at 9.40am in front of a small crowd. As soon as the starting signal was given, Prévot shot into the lead and set about carving out a fast pace. He made the first five kilometres in 18:13.2 and ten kilometres in 37:39.8 and had covered 15.5 kilometres by the end of the first hour. But Len had also made a solid start by covering 15.0 kilometres in the first hour. Prévot was still in the lead after two hours and, having covered 30.2 kilometres, was 750 metres ahead of Len and 900 metres ahead of Charbonnel, his closest rivals. In the third hour Prévot had to stop for a short massage and lost the lead to Edouard Cibot, winner of this year's Paris-Conflans Marathon, who covered 40 kilometres in 2:45:09.4 and 43.5 kilometres in three hours. Len was unable to follow the fast pace that Cibot was setting but was still well placed in the race with 42.0 kilometres after three hours. In the fourth hour, however, he lost a lot more ground and had to watch as Cibot lowered his 50-kilometre world

The runners line up on the grass track at Buffalo for the 50-mile race. Left to right: Victor Bagré, Georges Fleury, Edouard Cibot, Henri Prévot, Gustave Thomas, Albert Charbonnel and Len Hurst sharing a few words with his attendant.

In the early stages of the race, the pace is set by Henri Prévot, who is seen here leading from Len Hurst and Albert Charbonnel.

Len Hurst and his great French rival Albert Charbonnel after an hour of racing.

Len Hurst devant Cibot, à la cinquième heure.

Showing good track etiquette, Len makes space to let Cibot through on the inside shortly before retiring in the fifth hour.

record to 3:32:47.4. All the same, he had covered 52.5 kilometres in four hours and was still lying in third place. During the next hour, however, everything fell apart. He tried walking pauses, but nothing helped and so he had to give up completely exhausted after 56.5 kilometres. What had gone wrong? The *Sporting Life* provided the answer: he 'was out of sorts and want of training told the tale'. As Len dragged himself off to the dressing room his old rival Gustave Thomas swept into the lead and ran out an easy winner in a world-record time of 6:13.29.2.

It's a pity that such an outstanding year should have ended on such a low note, but he could look back on a superlative campaign capped by

a record-breaking win in the iconic London to Brighton race and a 25-mile track world record to add to his other records. He didn't compete in the Paris-Conflans Marathon that year, but his record of three wins, two seconds and one third between 1896 and 1902 would remain unsurpassed as the event was discontinued in 1904. During its short lifespan the

Paris-Conflans Marathon had been the world's premier marathon race, outstripping the rival Boston Marathon in terms of participation levels and quality.

As a world-class long-distance runner, Len was clearly not one for doing things in half measures. The 50-mile race at Buffalo brought it home that he no longer had the time to do the training necessary to stay at the top of his game and that the only logical consequence was to retire from competition. Once he had crossed this Rubicon, he was able to focus his energies on the running of his pub rather than races. As a long-time professional runner, he knew only too well what it took – and the sacrifices that had to be made – to get to the top and stay there. His working-class background has instilled in him the belief that hard work begot success and that nothing worth having ever came easily. The work ethic that had fuelled his competitive fire would also help him achieve his ambitious goals as an innkeeper. Like the 'Golden Eagle' in his native Sittingbourne, his pub was to be a meeting place for sports enthusiasts. One of his first orders of business was to sit down with some well-known sportsmen in the autumn of that year to discuss arrangements for the formation of the East London Professional Athletic & Cycling Club. Upwards of 40 members attended the first meeting at its new headquarters, the Turner's Arms. The club initially only promoted professional athletics and cycling, but later boxing was added, necessitating a change of name to the 'East London Professional Association'.

THE LATER YEARS

Despite all its efforts, the newly formed East London Professional Association was unable to generate as much interest in its promotions as had been hoped and soon folded. One of its main problems, no doubt, was that their president was unable to represent his organisation at its own meetings because, of course, he was busy getting his pub off the ground and unable to put in the requisite training. Nevertheless, the challenges kept on coming until even the persistent Charlie Hart realised that his nemesis would not be returning to action any time soon.

In 1904 Len left the Turner's Arms and moved to the Lord Napier at 39 Collingwood Street in Bethnal Green, where he would stay for the next ten years. Although there are no traces of the Lord Napier (later renamed The Victory) in Collingwood Street today, it was presumably at a more favourable location and would have been better appointed than the Turner's Arms. It was around this time that Len must have had his first flyer made. A surviving copy of one is shown on the previous page. He would have distributed it to sporting friends and at sporting events in order to promote his new premises. It featured a photo of himself wearing his prized champion belt and a not-entirely-error-free list of his 'best performances'. It was also 'recyclable': when he moved, he could quickly paste the name of the new restaurant over the free corner at the bottom left.

The next few years saw Len spending more and more time behind the bar and less and less time outdoors. The unholy trinity of inactivity, food and drink would inevitably take its toll on his waistline so that within just a few years of becoming an innkeeper his weight would balloon to an unsportsmanlike 13 stone 7 pounds, or 98 kilogrammes in modern units.

However, in 1907 there were some signs that Len had resumed training, although we do not know how often he was getting out and how much training he was doing. At any rate, word got around that he was exercising regularly again.

In July the *Sporting Life* announced that the French newspaper *L'Auto* had sent him 300 francs to cover his expenses so that he could take part in a race from Paris to Rouen in September. He duly made the trip to Paris and toed the starting line but was forced to pull out after five kilometres due, it was reported, to 'knee trouble'.

Shortly after, anyhow, Len was challenged by Andrew Johnson of Rochdale, to run 30 miles for the Championship of England and a purse of £100. Johnson's backer also put his money where his mouth was by placing a deposit of £10 with the *Sporting Life* in late October. Len promptly covered the deposit, and the match was on. As per the rules it was to be decided at the Rochdale within six to eight weeks from the signing of articles. The date was set at 28 December 1907, which coincided with Len's 36th birthday. The terms of the match weren't really in Len's favour because he was not in shape, carrying too much weight and facing a formidable opponent in the form of his life. The match had all the makings of a one-sided affair and yet the interest was there somehow. Johnson's backers must have evidently thought that dismantling the great Len Hurst would enhance their protégé's image. The roles were clearly defined: Johnson, the up-and-coming challenger; Len, the old champion making a last bid for glory. Despite facing certain defeat and the real prospect of humiliation, Len stepped into the ring. Was he fooling himself? Or did he just miss standing in the limelight or reliving the intoxicating thrill of the big match?

Who was this upstart anyway? Johnson was 31 years old age and a master window cleaner. A former amateur, he had represented Rochdale Harriers and, latterly, Salford Harriers, for whom he finished tenth in the 1904 Northern Cross-Country Championship. On Saturday, 30 June 1907 he had defeated Jess Hodgkinson over ten miles at Rochdale Athletic Ground in a very respectable 54:28.5. Johnson was such an overwhelming favourite, in fact, that only small number of spectators bothered to brave the chilly weather and watch the race.

Even from the very beginning it was clear that Len could not match his opponent's pace. After the first lap had been completed, Johnson had a lead of 50 yards which he steadily extended, lapping Len after three miles and again after seven miles. Johnson covered the first ten miles in 1:00:10, while Len took four minutes longer. Again and again, Len was lapped until he finally retired at 19 ½ miles (31.3 kilometres) in about two hours 14 minutes. That wouldn't have been a bad performance per

Andrew Johnson from Rochdale inflicted a heavy defeat on Len Hurst in late 1907.

se, but it was light years away from the times Len used to run. Johnson had inflicted upon him a defeat even more crushing than the one he himself had inflicted upon Bob Hallen several years earlier. As befitted a pro match, Len quickly gave Johnson permission to stop, which the latter duly did after completing 21 ½ miles in 2:15:30.

This sobering defeat by Andrew Johnston was a real body blow and would have been anything but the perfect bookend to a great career, but, as fate would have it, Len would get another chance to bow out in style. Twelve years after the first games of the modern Olympiad had unexpectedly opened the door to the world of marathon running for him and transformed his career, he would get the opportunity to bring that career to a fitting conclusion before a home crowd in the aftermath of the London Olympic Games. The Games of 1908 had captivated an entire nation and the track and field competitions at the new Olympic stadium at the White City exhibition grounds had been especially well received. However, one event put everything else in the shade: the Marathon Race from Windsor Castle to The Stadium, an epic 26.2-mile struggle that cut a path of broken bodies across London under the gaze of an estimated one million spectators. The course had had to be extended a few times so it could start at the royal residence in Windsor and finish in front of the royal box at the stadium. The original plan was to run 25 miles, but in the end it was 26 miles 385 yards, which has been the officially recognised distance for marathons since 1921. The additional yards that had to be added to the course would be the undoing of the supposed winner. After two hours 45 minutes of running on dusty roads under a blazing sun, a lone figure, the diminutive Italian champion Dorando Pietri, staggered into the stadium to deafening cheers and applause a mile ahead of the next runner. As soon as he had stepped onto the huge cinder track, however, the drama began to unfold. About 350 yards from the finishing post across the stadium, where Princess Alexandria anxiously awaited the victor, Pietri keeled over and crumpled to the ground. Only with the energetic help of the attending physician Dr Bulger did he manage to get up again and stagger onwards round the track. He collapsed four more times before finally lurching across the finish line into the waiting arms of attendants. At first Pietri was acclaimed as the winner, but the celebrations turned out to be premature. The Americans immediately lodged a protest for, as they argued, Pietri had received illicit assistance – a protest that was hard to deny given 80,000 witnesses. Pietri was disqualified and the gold medal given to the second man home, Johnny Hayes, who of course was an American. Nevertheless, this was an age when heroism trumped rules, and Pietri was regarded by many as the 'real' winner. While Hayes was politely applauded at the awards ceremony the following day, the Italian received a vociferous standing ovation when Princess Alexandria presented him with a gold cup to commemorate his plucky effort. After the Olympics both Hayes and Pietri turned professional and in New

York had a rematch, which the Italian won. The ensuing controversy and publicity triggered a marathon boom across the world. Every sportsman worth his salt wanted to prove that he could complete a marathon. In Great Britain, there was another backstory, though. A lot had been expected from the British representatives in the Olympic marathon, but all 12 of them had failed. The most highly placed Briton had finished 12th in a mediocre time over 20 minutes behind the winner. The British self-image was tarnished. With rehabilitation in mind, the *Evening News* took it upon itself to promote a marathon race for professionals over a near-identical route with the self-declared aim of proving that at least Britain's professional runners were among the best in the world. The result was a race that would go down in history. It had been expected that the race would attract a good number of participants, but not that so many professionals, veterans and retired champions of yesteryear would come forward. As the entries flooded in, the names on the list read like a 'Who's Who' of British pedestrianism. They included such unlikely candidates as former mile world-record holder Walter George, who at the time was 51 years of age. The *Daily Mail* reported, 'Although it is many years since he donned a running shoe, W.G. George ... proposes to run the race with the aid of oxygen.' Of course, Len could not miss this exciting opportunity. Even though he wasn't one of the top favourites, the *Evening News* made him their favourite and regularly reported on the progress of his training. After he had signed up for the race, Len placed himself in the capable coaching hands of 'Jolly Jumbo' Ecclestone,

Len is seen here disrobing for a training spin alongside his trainer Jolly Jumbo.

a 20-stone colossus of a man who rode alongside Len during his training spins on a horse-drawn gig dishing out instructions.

'I am up every morning at six o'clock and before breakfast I run four miles . Afterwards I do from eight to 12 miles before dinner, and then rest for an hour to two. In the afternoon and evening I go out again, and by nine o'clock I am in bed. I shall not have a trial run of the full distance. If I can run 15 miles I know I can run 50. I never ran 15 miles in my life, and for the Brighton race the biggest stretch I did was eight or nine miles. I went for good long walks, but I would sooner run ten miles than walk five.'
(London Evening News)

The readers of the *Evening News* learned that Len was putting in 27 miles a day of walking and running on the lanes around Kenton and

Kingsbury. His weight was back down to 11 stone 6 pounds (82 kg) and he had improved to around two hours ten minutes for 20 miles. His trainer, Mr. Ecclestone, had this to say: '*Although I do not say positively that he will win, yet I would be willing to guarantee that he is among the finishers. Hurst is going very well and is in capital condition. I know he has some very good men to meet, but if he is able to run to his scheduled time he will come out all right.*'

The hot favourite, however, was the 21-year-old French soldier Henri Siret, already a three-time winner of the Tour de Paris Marathon. Siret, a moderate smoker and drinker, had reportedly been running 15 to 20 miles a day and was confident of smashing the record. Much was also expected from Irish farmhand Pat White, who had won a 21¼ mile road race in Newry a year earlier in a very fast time of 1:59:43 on the

This photo was taken at Windsor just after the start of the 1908 Evening News Marathon and shows, among others, the leading Briton Jack Keywood (#77).

back of training that consisted solely of daily work on the fields and the occasional run of about ten miles a week.

On Saturday, 10 October 1908 the big day had finally arrived. 89 of the 124 pros whose entry had been accepted gathered at the Sovereign's Gate on the grounds of Windsor Castle and were sent on their way by Princess Victoria of Schleswig-Holstein. The pros, unlike their amateur brethren, had not been allowed to set off from the East Lawn of Windsor Castle or to enter the stadium through the same entrance either. This meant that the course had to be changed slightly so that, whether accidentally or intentionally, it was also a bit longer at 26 miles 585 yards.

Despite the longer distance, the cool autumn weather ensured a much faster race than that of the amateurs in the July afternoon heat. Siret lived up to his billing as favourite and won by nearly three minutes from Pat White in a then-spectacular time of 2:37:23. British eyes were also smiling on this occasion thanks to Jack Keywood, a tall, lean and heavily moustached master builder from Bromley who finished third in an excellent 2:41:19.8.

Neither existing images nor contemporary reports indicate that Len was prominently placed at any point in the race. He, of course, knew that he could not keep up with the front runners and was content to start at a conservative pace and work his way through the field. After only two months of training he managed to finish the race in 25th place and complete the course in 3:23:00.6 leaving several good runners behind. In an interview afterwards, however, he expressed disappointment at his performance and explained, by way of an excuse, that he had gone through a bad patch after being given what he thought was brandy by a spectator. Even though the newspapers had talked up his chances, Siret hadn't considered him a serious threat: *'I saw Len Hurst at the start, but he looked too heavy to be dangerous. I had my eye on Aldridge, Johnson, White and Smallwood.'* Len had done well to get fit enough to run a marathon within a few months, but there was absolutely no way he could get into the kind of shape he was when he was in his prime and feared by everyone.

So that was that. At the age of 37, Len hung up his racing shoes for good. He'd had a wonderful career and, it was reckoned, had earned around £30,000 over 20 years in prize money, side bets, expenses, percentages from backers and gate money, appearance money and endorsements. He'd had some good years and some bad years, but there was no doubting that professional running had served him well overall.

Two years later, when the marathon running boom was still in full swing, an international indoor 'Marathon Derby' for professionals was held at the Agricultural Hall in Islington. The starters were competing for a challenge belt whose centrepiece was a star with eight small medallions containing miniature photographs representing distance-running legends of yesteryear – Bill Lang, Jack White, Teddy Mills, George Hazael, John Fleet, Deerfoot and, the latest addition to the pantheon of long-distance greats, Len Hurst.

FACT OR FICTION?

In addition to his many records and triumphs, Len was particularly proud of his 'alternative' exploits. Although unverifiable, there are two which are especially worth mentioning. One was a claim that he could run ten miles and make 8,000 bricks within 12 hours – a feat tailor-made for Len as it uniquely combined his running abilities and his brickmaking skills.

His other claim to fame was defeating a cob horse in a 20-mile race on the road from Edmonton to Hoddeston and back. Races between horses and humans are not all that unusual, but horses are notoriously difficult to beat. Beating a horse at its own game was something people in the bygone days of horse-drawn transport could easily identify with. To put things into perspective, a so-called 'Man versus Horse Marathon' over 22 miles, held annually in the Welsh town of Llanwrtyd Wells since 1980, currently stands at 38 wins to two in favour of the equine competitor.

WHAT'S IN A NAME

Today the name Len Hurst is immortalised in connection with the Paris Marathon, which was first held in 1976, 40 years after his passing. The Paris Marathon website includes a historic timeline where Len is credited with winning the first Paris marathon race in 1896. The modern-day city marathon first emerged in the 1970s when the power of the media was harnessed for the first time to orchestrate gigantic televised marathons where the elite rubbed shoulders with the masses. Today, several city marathons, of which Paris is foremost, also have something intangible that is of immeasurable value: provenance. A sporting event with provenance, such as a marathon race that can trace its roots back to early times, is imbued with a special sense of historic worth and tradition. In Paris, that tradition began with Len Hurst.

THE FINAL CHAPTER

His marathon running days over, Len returned to his bread-winning day job of running a pub. In truth, his wife Ethel was the one in charge; she not only held the purse strings but also attended to the everyday running of the business, including serving drinks. Len was the gregarious type who preferred to spend his time in front of the bar regaling customers with stories from his eventful life as a brickmaker and professional runner.

Shortly before the outbreak of the First World War, Len transferred from the Lord Napier to the George IV Tavern at 68 Berner Street in Aldgate. When the ongoing war effort led to the introduction of compulsory military service in 1916, Len was comfortably over the maximum age limit for conscription. Nevertheless, the war was a difficult time for innkeepers. Strict licensing laws were imposed by the Central Control Board responsible for the sale and supply of 'intoxicating liquors'. In cities such as London, where munitions were produced on a large scale, restrictions were imposed on civil liberties and, for instance, the opening hours of public houses were drastically reduced to safeguard the efficiency of workers. There were no 'rounds': draconian punishments also awaited those who treated others to alcoholic beverages. As an additional deterrent for would-be drinkers, the government radically increased the tax on alcohol to generate much-needed revenues. As with most innkeepers, Len also saw his clientele dwindle over time, as more and more young men aged 18 to 40 were drafted into military service and sent to the front from which they were not to return.

When all is said and done, the travails of the publican during World War One bore no comparison to the horrors of the front line.

Even before the war began, all but one of Len's distance-running records had been wiped off the record books. When he retired from competitive sport, he still held all professional records from 13 to 25 miles. However, his records came under fire during the Marathon Craze between 1908 and 1910, when marathon running became a global phenomenon. Given the sheer number of track races over distances from ten to 26 miles, it was only a matter of time until someone came along and improved his records. His professional 25-mile record was eclipsed on 3 April 1909 when the prolific French runner Henri St. Yves lowered it to 2:32:11.6 at the Polo Ground near New York. The following month, St. Yves also improved the professional 20-mile record to 1:51:46 in another marathon race at the same venue. It seems that the news in those days travelled slowly across the Atlantic, because even in 1911 Len was still credited with all professional records from 13 to 25 miles in the *Sporting Chronicle Annual*.

Only the London to Brighton record remained in his name after the war. It wasn't until 1924 that a man capable of surpassing it emerged. His name: Arthur Francis Hamilton Newton. Newton, then a veteran of 41 years, had emigrated to South Africa to become a farmer but had returned to England in 1924 for a short stay, during which he hoped to beat the London to Brighton record. During the passage from Cape Town to Southampton he had kept fit by running a dizzying number of laps on the deck of the steamer. After the expropriation of his land in Natal, Newton had taken up running in the hope that his success would provide him with a platform to draw the South African government's attention to his cause. Starting from scratch as an absolute beginner, he entered the 1922 Comrades Marathon, a gruelling 54-mile race between Pietermaritzburg and Durban. To cut a long story short, he succeeded in winning but failed to get the government to budge on the land resettlement issue. However, he had caught the running bug and soon developed into a world-class long-distance runner. Newton, a member of Thames Hare and Hounds, owed his success to ascetic self-discipline allied to an insatiable appetite for training. In 1923 he ran and walked an average of 25 miles a day. In the late 1920s he turned professional and set world records for 24 hours and 100 miles. Later he wrote articles about running and a total of four mostly anecdotal books with his unorthodox views and advice, which were to inspire a whole generation of long-distance runners to new heights. Today, Newton is widely regarded as the father of LSD – not the mind-expanding drug, but 'Long Slow Distance' running, a term irreverently coined in 1969 by the American writer Joe Henderson.

The Brighton route had changed a bit in the years since Len's day. In the early 1920s, the road was straightened and tarmacadamed, making it faster if not shorter. Newton prepared himself for his record attempt

This picture was taken on 3 October 1924 after Arthur Newton's first solo run from London to Brighton. Len Hurst and other famous old timers offer congratulations. Left to right: Joe Binks, Len Hurst, Arthur Newton and Jimmy Fowler Dixon.

on 3 October 1924 by racking up 830 miles in August and 702 miles in September, before tapering down to an 'easy' 20 miles of running a day in the preceding weeks. Despite being a former professional, Len was invited to accompany Newton in a car with Joe Binks, athletics correspondent at *News of the World*, and Jimmy Fowler, Dixon and Tony Fattorini as official A.A.A. timekeepers. When he saw Newton's seemingly effortless, shuffling gait, Len was amazed and exclaimed, 'This fellow will run until Christmas.' Despite the improved roads, it was not until the final stages of the run that Newton was able to get ahead of Len's intermediate times set over two decades earlier. In the last part of the run, however, where Len had taken walking breaks, Newton made significant gains and improved the course record to 6:11:04.4.

Len, as befits a true gentleman, was one of the first to congratulate Newton on his achievement. Len was full of admiration for Newton's performance. Yet Newton was dissatisfied with his run. Apart from lingering doubts that he hadn't broken the old record convincingly enough in view of the better weather and paved roads, he felt he had failed to do himself justice. Having done all his running on dirt roads in South Africa, Newton was well qualified to appreciate the relative merits of his performance and that of his predecessor. He therefore decided to make another attempt and put the issue beyond doubt. The following month he made his next attempt, which this time was made in the absence of the former course record holder, who, no doubt, would have given Newton his best wishes. Battling through wet and windy conditions, Newton produced a phenomenal run to complete the course in a sensational time of 5:53:43. During the run he also set world-record figures for 50 miles of 5:38:42. With his marathon split of 2:42:52, he would have won the silver medal at the Olympic Games a few months earlier. At the time there was only a handful of Britons capable of beating three hours for the marathon, let alone two consecutive marathons in less than six hours. Immediately after the finish, Newton lit up his trademark pipe and walked off smilingly to the dressing room. Despite the presence of time-honoured officials Jimmy Fowler-Dixon and Tony Fattorini, however, the sticklers at the A.A.A. refused to recognise Newton's record unless the course was measured beyond doubt.

The press coverage of Arthur Newton's record-breaking London to Brighton runs in 1924 would see the spotlight fall on Len Hurst for one last time. His outright course record had lasted 21 years, but his professional record would not be beaten during his lifetime.

After the war, the Hursts moved around a bit. First, they transferred from the George IV Tavern to The Bee Hive in Notting Hill, and then in 1923 to The Eagle in Farringdon Road, Clerkenwell.

When he had the time, Len would bring a barrel of beer to the Edmonton Brickfields where he and Joe would organise a race for the brickfield workers. Joe continued to work in the brickfields where, later in life, he had four of his sons working with him. He finally retired a few years before his death in 1940 at the age of 82.

Len remained an avid follower of athletics after his retirement but was

also interested in boxing (his son Leonard Jnr. was a notable amateur boxer). He was often to be seen at the Blackfriars Ring, a popular boxing and wrestling venue that was knocked out by a bomb in 1940. He was a great friend of the M.C. George Harris, and Jim Kenrick, one of the referees, as well as Len

Joe Hurst, pictured here around 1920.

Harvey. Kenrick and Harris always wanted to introduce him from the ring, but Len always declined, anxious to avoid personal publicity. An astute businessman and showman, he remained a self-effacing individual who never sought the trappings of celebrity and fame. It was the same at athletics meetings at the White City, where he was always content to be an ordinary spectator. When he attended meetings at Stamford Bridge, he always went to the terraces, but usually an official would recognise him and insist that he take a seat in the stands. The only time he came out of his shell of diffidence was to defend his reputation. In 1921 an article appeared in *All Sports Illustrated Weekly* penned by Charlie Hart as part of his serialised life story 'Forty years a runner'. In the article Hart claimed that although Len had won the Fifteen Hours' Championship he had collapsed a few yards from the tape and had been helped over the line. Len threatened to sue for libel, as this was patently untrue. *All Sports Illustrated Weekly* apologised, stopped the series and settled the matter out of court. Len was then asked by the magazine to write his life story. A reporter visited him a couple of times but found him reluctant to talk. Len's son Alfred made no mention of any memoirs or the like. This diffidence is perhaps one reason why Len Hurst is less famous today than he otherwise might have been. One wonders what he would have made of this story.

In the early 1930s, the Hursts took over The Neptune in Clarendon Street, Somers Town, about half a mile from Kings Cross Station. It was a great location and a well-frequented public house, the culmination of nigh-on three decades in the licensed victualling business.

In the 1930s the Hursts ran The Neptune in Clarendon Street, Somers Town.

Unfortunately, the pub no longer exists, but at the time of writing the original building was still on the corner where Werrington Street intersects with Cranleigh Street. The only pub still in operation and once run by

Len Hurst is The Eagle in Clerkenwell. However, The Neptune was not licensed to Leonard Hurst, but for the first time to Caroline Ethel Hurst. Was this a first sign that something was wrong? Indeed. Drinking was an occupational hazard for publicans in those days, as they were expected to drink with their customers. As someone who liked to socialise, Len was particularly at risk. In the early 1930s, his health began to deteriorate after the onset of liver cirrhosis. With no welfare state to provide support, Ethel continued to run the pub while tending to her ailing husband. The children provided indispensable help, but it was obvious that their father was, for once, battling an opponent whom he could not defeat. A great

The Hurst family grave and the final resting place of Len Hurst at Manor Park Cemetery in East London (courtesy of Ian Champion).

sadness was felt in the sporting community, in London and in his native Sittingbourne when Len Hurst passed away on 22 November 1937 at the age of 65. He was laid to rest at the Manor Park Cemetery in Forest Gate, where a large congregation of grieving family, friends and acquaintances came to pay their last respects to 'their' champion.

After the death of her husband, Ethel lived comfortably in Hanwell, Middlesex, until her death in 1955 at the age of 78. Before she died, however, she would make a gesture of generosity that would guarantee her late husband's legacy.

THE LEN HURST LEGACY

In the early 1950s the Hurst family decided that they would like to put the champion belt Len had won to some use as a memorial to him. To this end they approached Joe Binks, the doyen of athletic journalists, who was still working for the *News of the World*. He suggested presenting it to the newly formed Road Runners Club (RRC) as a trophy for the London to Brighton race, first held in 1951, and a race close to Len's heart. The Hursts agreed and in 1953 the belt was presented to the winning team for the first time by Alfred Hurst, Len's youngest son.

Before the belt could be accepted, since it had been a professional trophy, permission had to be given by the amateur athletics authorities for it to be used as a trophy in an amateur race. This permission was eventually secured and the belt was officially presented to the RRC on 10 May 1953 by Mrs Len Hurst. Rex Cross, the then President of the RRC, then gave it back to Mrs Hurst to present to the winning team of 1952, Blackheath Harriers. The belt was in poor repair at that point and so it was sent to the Royal School of Needlework at Hampton Court Palace which specialised in the restoration of historic needlework.

After being repaired, the belt was put in a special case by the RRC. The previous engraving on the silver badges on the belt was erased, not a difficult job with sterling silver. The wording 'The Len Hurst Belt' was engraved on the central shield and the RRC logo on two of the side badges.

The central shield of the 'Len Hurst Belt'.

As one of the few professional running-belt trophies from the heyday of the pedestrian era during Queen Victoria's reign, it was presented each year to the winning club team in the London to Brighton race until the race was discontinued.

The famous 'Len Hurst Belt' has an intriguing history. The sterling silver badges and shields, which are such a striking feature, were made by the Birmingham silversmiths Hillard and Thomason, with an assay marking dating them to 1885. It would seem that around 1900 the main badge at the front and a side shield were damaged, and these two silver sections were replaced by another Birmingham silversmiths, Vaughton & Sons, in 1901, prior to the belt being won by Len Hurst. The belt was actually referred to by Len as the G. & S. Belt after London silversmiths and jewellers Goldsmiths & Silversmiths Co. but had no G. & S. assay markings. The champion belt was therefore by no means new when it was awarded to Len in 1902. How Tom Connor, proprietor of the Old Bow Running Grounds, came into possession of the belt is not known. The Sporting Life report on the ten-mile handicap refers to a gold and silver belt, but in fact the badges were entirely made of silver. Its origin is a mystery, but obviously it has a history and it probably originated in the Midlands around 1885. To make things even more complicated, it was possibly not even originally a running belt, but perhaps a boxing belt that was subsequently modified. Pedestrian belts such as the Len Hurst Belt have a long history. The first ten-mile champion belt was awarded in 1852 to a runner named George Frost. Later in the 1850s there was a famous series of races between the leading runners of the period, William Jackson and John Levett, where the belt changed hands several times. In 1882 the Scotsman William Cummings twice won the ten-mile belt in races at Lillie Bridge in London. This belt had been presented by Sir John Astley and was almost certainly a different belt to that originally awarded in 1852. The Astley ten-mile belt was apparently not at stake in Cummings's two famous races with Walter George, in 1885 and 1886. What happened to the belt after that is unknown.

The probable original cost of the original belt was around £50 in 1893, which today would equate to a retail value of over £6,000. Vaughton & Sons, who repaired the belt in 1901, still exist as part of a larger firm.

The above photo shows the presentation made on 10 May 1953 at Surbiton Town Sports Club in Riverhill, Surrey. On the extreme left, with glasses, is Ernest Neville, founder of RRC. The second seated man in the grey suit is Edgar Lloyd, former holder of the amateur 50-mile world record; standing behind and to his right in the black suit is Rex Cross, first President of the RRC. Which of the two seated ladies is Mrs Len Hurst is not known, but it is more likely to be the elderly lady left of centre. Seated between them is Derek Reynolds, 1952 Brighton winner, who accepted the belt on behalf of Blackheath Harriers 1952 team race winners. The man with the glasses and moustache behind and to right of the seated lady in the white coat is Dr Harold Lee FRCS (third in 1951 in Brighton). To his right stands Sam Ferris, renowned GB international and 1932 Olympic Marathon silver medallist. Seated in front of him is 'the legend' Arthur Newton. It is not known which cup Reynolds is holding, but it is possibly the Edgar Lloyd Cup. The belt in the case resting on Reynolds's knees is, of course, the Len Hurst Belt.

In 1999 they were able to quote a price for making a copy of the Len Hurst belt today. They estimated that a modern replica would cost close to £3,500. That figure would be around £8,000 now given the increase in the value of silver since then.

The iconic landmarks of London and along the route, the international flair, the rich history of the race and the impressive list of winners were just some of the things that made the London to Brighton so special for so many for so long. For the lucky winner and the lucky winning team there was the opportunity to hold for one year the Arthur Newton Cup, the prestigious trophy once held aloft by Arthur Newton, and the coveted Len Hurst Belt once worn by 'the man' himself. Many of the past presidents of the Road Runners' Club (an office typically held for two years) were themselves marathon and ultra-running icons, like for example 1932 Olympic Marathon silver medallist Sam Ferris, 1970 Commonwealth Marathon Champion Ron Hill and world 100 kilometre record holder Don Ritchie. Each president was responsible for the custody of the Arthur Newton Cup and the Len Hurst Belt, which, as one can imagine, must have passed through the hands of many great runners and celebrities over the years.

The race from London to Brighton was one of the world's leading ultra-marathons for many years and brought together the best ultra-runners in the world. Before the IAU 100 kilometre World Championship was founded in 1987, it was considered an unofficial World Ultramarathon Championship and was typically won by either British or South African runners. The distance varied over the years, but generally became longer over time, mainly due to the expansion of Gatwick Airport. As a result, there are several course records, with the most impressive performances being the South African Bruce Fordyce's 5:12:32 in 1983 over a distance of 53 miles 1082 yards and that of Luton's 1974 Commonwealth Marathon Champion Ian Thompson who won the 1980 race in 5:15:15 after covering 54 miles 460 yards. The men's race record was set in 1972, when Scotland's Alastair Wood clocked 5:11:00 over a course measuring

This photograph shows the 1997 London to Brighton team winners Crawley Athletic Club proudly holding the Len Hurst Belt. L-R: Mayor of Brighton, Betty Walshe; Rob Sharp, Walter Hill and Dave Beattie.

52 miles 1172 yards; and the women's in 1993, when England's Carolyn Hunter finished in 6:34:10 over a course measuring exactly 55 miles. Len would have been flabbergasted that one day a woman would come along and beat his Brighton record. In 1936, the year before his death, the 100 metre sprint was the longest race track women were allowed to run at the Berlin Olympic Games.

There was no question that the London to Brighton was a very popular event due to its unique route, but unfortunately this route would also be its undoing. Traffic was light in the early years but became increasingly heavier over time as the capital expanded south and more and more towns were sucked into the London Commuter Belt. This ultimately led to the race becoming increasingly dangerous for both competitors and marshals alike. The Road Runners' Club were proud of the fact that in the 55-year history of the race not a single competitor had come to harm due to a collision with a motor vehicle. From 2000 onwards the route had to be altered nearly every year due to new construction works. According to RRC President and chief race organiser Ian Champion, the race had become a bit of a gamble, an, quote, 'accident waiting to happen'. In 2005, after years of to and fro, the RRC finally decided with a heavy heart to discontinue the race and finish on their own terms and with a clean record. Roll on 14 years, and the Arthur Newton Cup is still in the possession of the RRC but the Len Hurst Belt is not. That's because it has found a new home. In 2018 it was ceremoniously presented to nine-time team winners Crawley Athletic Club and has since been on permanent display at the Crawley AC Museum.

LEN HURST'S BEST PERFORMANCES

Distance	Performance	Venue	Date	Notes
4 miles	20:26.0	Sittingbourne	August 3, 1896	track race
6 miles	31:24.0+	Southampton	June 30, 1900	during 10-mile track race
10,000 m	34:43.4+	Paris	July 20, 1902	during 1-hour race
10 miles	53:20e	Sittingbourne	August 7, 1899	track race
1 hour	17,757m (11M 60y)	Bolton	April 16, 1898	during 20 miles
15 miles	1:22:21	Bolton	April 16, 1898	during 20 miles
20 miles	1:53:42.3	Wood Green	October 6, 1900	track race
25 miles	2:33:42	Preston Park, Brighton	August 27, 1903	track race
42503m (26M 722y)	3:00:00+	Paris	August 5, 1900	during 6-hour track race
Marathon	3:23:00.6	London	October 10, 1908	26M 585y
50K	3:35:45	Vincennes, FRA	August 5, 1900	during 6h track race
50 miles track	6:53:15	Stamford Hill	March 23, 1903	during 15h track race
50 miles road	6:16:12+	London-Brighton	June 20, 1903	50.5 miles

RACES

21.05.1888	Gore Court Park, Sittingbourne. 4-mile handicap (4 laps start). 2nd. £1 10s. 1-mile handicap (230 yds). Unplaced.
03.08.1888	Gore Court Park, Sittingbourne. 10-mile handicap. (1320y start). 5th.
10.06.1889	Gore Court Park, Sittingbourne. 4-mile handicap (880y start). 1st. £3. 10-mile handicap 5th. 7s. 6d.
12.04.1890	White Hart Running Grounds, Tottenham Hale. 5-mile handicap (650y start). Unplaced.
18.05.1891	Gore Court Park, Sittingbourne. 6-mile handicap (560y start). 4th. 10/0. Joe Hurst won in 34:00 off 50y.
03.08.1891	Gore Court Park, Sittingbourne. 6-mile handicap (570y start). 5th. Unplaced in mile hcp off 145y.
06.06.1892	Brown's Grounds, Nunhead. 1-hour GAYP handicap. 1st (off scratch). 10M 40y. Won timepiece and money prize.
06.06.1892	Sittingbourne. 6-mile handicap. 570y start, DNF.

15.08.1892	Old Bow Running Grounds. 5-mile handicap, also-ran off 300 yards.
10.09.1892	Old Bow Running Grounds. 880y handicap (75y start). DNF.
03.10.1892	Old Bow Running Grounds. 1-hour go-as-you-please handicap. 3 ½ laps start [948 y] with 6 ½ laps to the mile. 1st. 68 ¾ laps [10M 67y net]. £2.
23.10.1892	Old Bow Running Grounds. Bow Pedestrian Company 4-mile handicap. 4th off 350y.
07.11.1892	Old Bow Running Grounds. 4-mile handicap sweepstakes. 2nd off 350y. H. Batchelor (420y start) won by 5y.
12.12.1892	Old Bow Running Grounds. 3 hours handicap. 6 ½ laps to the mile. 9 ¾ laps start (1M 872y). 1st. £10. Hurst was awarded the race after covering 26M 1350y [25M 478y net] in 2:42 (acc. to The Sportsman) or 2:43:20 (acc. to SPL). Splits (net distance): 1h-10 ¼ miles; 1.5h-15M 207y; 2h-19M 1495y; 20M-2:01; 25M-2:40
28.01.1893	Prince of Wales Ground, Poplar. 4-mile handicap. 3rd off 100 y. 1 – Arthur Norris (scratch); 2 – Joe Hurst (200 y).
20.02.1893	Excelsior Baths, Bethnal Green. Six-day race, 12 hours per day. Day 1: 79.9 miles. Track was 11y short per lap. 2nd.
21.02.1893	Excelsior Baths, Bethnal Green. Six-day race, 12 hours per day. Day 2: 118.3 miles reported (DNF). 10th.
27.03.1893	Excelsior Baths, Bethnal Green. 30-mile handicap. 2nd. No times taken.
05.04.1893	Excelsior Baths, Bethnal Green. 4-mile handicap. 2nd. 1 – Joe Palmer (1 lap start); 2 – Len Hurst (1 ½ laps start) 17 y; 3 – Arthur Norris (scratch) 20 y
22.05.1893	Gore Court Park, Sittingbourne. Whit Monday meeting. Att.: 7000. 6-mile handicap. 1, 34:10 C. Kingsnorth (Sittingbourne, 420 y start) £5; 2, Len Hurst (370y start) in 34:12e (10 yds) £2.
26.08.1893	Edmonton. Meadow, Silver Street. 1-mile handicap. 2nd off 20 yards.
23.09.1893	Old Bow Running Grounds. 4-mile handicap. Heat 2. 2nd off 140 yds.
01.10.1893	Old Bow Running Grounds. 4-mile handicap final. 1 – W. Bishop (40y start); 2 – Len Hurst (140y behind) + Joe Hurst (140y behind) (the Hurst bros. dead-heated).
29.10.1893	White Hart Grounds, Tottenham Hale. 4-mile handicap. 1st off 75y (virtual scratch). Time: 20:51.0.
06.11.1893	Old Bow Running Grounds. 10-mile handicap. 3rd off scratch in 58:15e. 1, 56:30 Jem Bailey (4 laps start); 2, S. Stokes (3 ½ laps start), 250y; 3, Len Hurst (scratch) 200y. £1. Len Hurst: 5M-26:26

27.11.1893	Old Bow Running Grounds. 20 miles against A.E. Ware, of Camden Town for £10. Won easily. Ware, who had a 440y start, retired in the 11th mile and Hurst was given permission to stop at 12 miles in 1:08:38. 1M-5:21, 2M-10:40, 3M-16:10.5, 4M-21:35, 5M-27:08, 6M-32:30, 7M-38:23, 8M-45:10, 9M-51:09, 10M-57:03, 11M-1:02:58.
02.12.1893	Excelsior Baths, Bethnal Green. 20 miles against William Bealey (1 mile start) for £10 a-side. Aborted due to crowd invasion of running track.
26.12.1893	Old Bow Running Grounds. 4-mile handicap. 2nd off 120y. A lap scoring error resulted in first place being awarded to Ricketts (600y start).
23.03.1894	Invicta Grounds, Plumstead. 4-mile handicap. Hurst (scratch) was 7th.
14.05.1894	Sittingbourne, Gore Court Park, 4-mile handicap (80y start). 1st off 880y in 21:20. £5. Half-mile handicap: 1st heat 2 off 70y in 2:10.0. Won 10s for winning heat. Unplaced in final.
03.06.1894	Old Luke's Running Ground, Canning Town. 4-mile handicap. Hurst (scratch) retired after finding he could not overhaul the men with long starts.
10.06.1894	White Hart Grounds, Tottenham Hale. 10-mile handicap. 8 laps to mile. 2nd in 55:10e. 1 – Ted Shepherd (Higham), 550y start, 54:36, £6 10s; 2 – Len Hurst (scratch) 170y behind, £2; 3 – T. Perkins (Brompton), 170y start, £1 Hurst: 3M-15:15
16.06.1894	Alma Field, Enfield Lock. 1-mile handicap. 2nd off 90 yards. 16 started.
17.06.1894	Old Bow Running Grounds. 4-mile handicap. 4th off 50y.
25.06.1894	Old Bow Running Grounds. 1-mile handicap. 2nd heat 1 off 160y.
02.07.1894	Old Bow Running Grounds. 1-mile handicap. 3rd off 160y.
08.07.1894	White Hart Grounds, Tottenham Hale. 220 yards weight-carrying competition (bag of sand weighing 112 lb). Heat 4: walked over. Unplaced in semi-final.
10.07.1894	Edmonton. Meadow, opposite Bell Inn. Unplaced in half-mile and-mile handicaps.
06.08.1894	Sittingbourne. 4-mile handicap. 1st off 70y in 21:30. £5.
16.09.1894	Old Bow Running Grounds. 4-mile handicap. 3rd in heat 1 off 50 yds. First 3 to run in final.
23.09.1894	Old Bow Running Grounds. 4-mile handicap final. 3rd off 50 yds. Prize money 2s. 6d. 1 – Joe Hurst (1200y start); 2 – W. Cullingham (400y) 10y; 3 – Len Hurst (50y) 100y; 4 – Jem Bailey (400y)
22.10.1894	Brown's Grounds, Nunhead. 10 miles against Guy Temple of Southwark for £30. Won easily in 58:24.0. Heavy grass track.

14.11.1894	Excelsior Baths, Bethnal Green. Four Days' Thirty hours 'Go As You Please' race with the winner to receive a jewelled silver champion belt and £15. Hurst covered 25.35 miles in 3 hours (3).
15.11.1894	ditto. 3h – 21.35 miles (4 p.m.); 9h – 54.35 miles (79.7M) (2nd)
16.11.1894	ditto. 9h – 55.9 miles (135.6M) (1st)
17.11.1894	ditto. 9h – 49.2 miles (184.8M) (2nd). £8.
20.10.1895	Old Bow Running Grounds. 4-mile handicap. Retd. at 2 miles.
27.10.1895	Old Clay Hall Athletic Grounds, Old Ford Road, Bow. 150y track [SPL 13.11.1894]. 4-mile handicap. Retd. in the 3rd mile (scratch).
03.12.1895	Excelsior Baths, Bethnal Green. Four day twenty hours 'Go As You Please' contest for £20 in prize money. 10s. entrance fee. 1h – 9.5M (1); 2h – 17.4M (2); 3h – 25.15M (1); 5h – 38.4M (1)
04.12.1895	ditto. 1h – 8.3M (46.7M); 2h – 16.2M (54.6M); 3h – 23.4M (61.8M); 5h 36.0M – (74.4M). 1st
05.12.1895	ditto. 2h – 14.2M (89.6M); 4h – 27.7M (102.1M); 5h – 34.0M (108.4M). 1st
06.12.1895	ditto. 2h – 13.7M (122.1M), 5h – 30.4M (138 miles 15 laps). 1st
03.04.1896	Brown's Grounds, Nunhead. Great All England Four Mile Sweepstakes. 2nd. 1, Harry Anstead (Greenwich) 20:26.5 (£24); 2, Len Hurst 20:34.0e (40 y) £5, 3, George Tincler (Edinburgh); 4, J.G. James (Islington). Splits: 1M-5:04.5, 2M-10:12.5, 3M-15:18, 4M-20:34e
10.05.1896	Old Clay Hall Athletic Grounds, Bow. 4-mile handicap. 1st off scratch. No times taken.
23.05.1896	Gore Court Park, Sittingbourne. 4-mile handicap. 2nd off 100 yds. Harry Anstead (scratch) won by 40 yards.
31.05.1896	Old Bow Running Grounds. 4-mile handicap. 1st off 100y (virtual scratch). Won a gold medal.
19.07.1896	Paris-Conflans Marathon. 40 km. 1st in 2:31:29.8. F2000.
01.08.1896	Buffalo Velodrome, Paris-Neuilly. 1-hour match against Henri Mathlin. Won by 600m with 16580m. 5 km - 17:13.4, 10 km – 35:41.6. Continued to 17 km (1:01:28).
03.08.1896	Gore Court Park, Sittingbourne. 4 miles 1st in 20:26.0. Mile handicap 1st off 96 yds. in 4:41.0
08.08.1896	Buffalo Velodrome, Paris-Neuilly. 20,000m against Albert Chauvelot. Won by 150 m in 1:12:44.4. 5 km - 16:58.8, 6 km - 20:30.0, 7 km - 24:03.2, 8 km - 27.48.2, 9 km - 31:32.4, 10 km - 35:00.4, 11 km – 38:39.4, 12 km - 42:19, 13 km - 45:57, 14 km - 49:42.2, 15 km - 53:41.4, 16 km - 57:34.2, 1h – 16,612m, 17 km - 1:01:30, 18 km - 1:05:25.8, 19 km – 1:09:02.8.
22.08.1896	O'Ryan's Field, Ponder's End. 1-mile open handicap. Off scratch. 2nd.
16.04.1897	Brown's Grounds, Nunhead. 4-mile handicap. 2nd off 85y. £1 10s.

30.05.1897	Old Bow Running Grounds. 4-mile handicap. 1st from scratch. No times taken.
15.06.1897	King's Head grounds, Edmonton. 10-mile exhibition match against Joe Hurst. 1st. 58:28.0. 17 laps + 60y to the mile.
24.07.1897	Ewood Park, Blackburn. 20 miles against Watkins for £200. Won. Watkins retired at 14¾ miles. Hurst was given permission to stop at 15¼ miles in 1:27:12. 1M – 5:07, 2M – 10:25, 3M – 15:47, 4M – 21:17, 5M – 26:58, 6M – 32:40, 7M – 38:34, 8M – 44:10, 9M – 49:56, 10M – 55:50, 11M – 1:02:04, 12M – 1:08:36, 13M – 1:14:08, 14M – 1:20:03, 15M – 1:25:43.
02.08.1897	Sittingbourne. 1-mile handicap 1st off 75y 4:50; 4-mile handicap 1st off 50y 21:30.
29.08.1897	Old Bow Running Grounds (morning). 4-mile handicap. 1st from scratch. No times taken.
29.08.1897	Edmonton (afternoon). 1-mile handicap. 33 entrants. 3rd off scratch (Joe Hurst won off 125 yds).
30.08.1897	Lower Edmonton. King's Head Grounds. 1-mile handicap. 3rd off scratch. No times taken.
13.09.1897	Oddfellows' Fete. Chase Side House Grounds. Enfield.
24.10.1897	Old Bow Running Grounds. Attendance: 1300. 10-mile handicap. Scratch. Retired in 7th mile.
04.12.1897	Old Bow Running Grounds. 4-mile handicap. 4th off scratch.
05.02.1898	Rochdale. 10 miles against George Crossland for £200. Won in 54:02.5. 1M-5:19 (Crossland), 2M-10:20 (Crossland), 3M-15:42.6 (Hurst), 4M-21:09 (Crossland), 5M-26:42.4 (Crossland), 6M-32:07 (Crossland), 6½M-34:35.2 (Hurst), 7M-37:30 (Hurst), 7½M-40:27.5 (Hurst), 8M-43:15 (Hurst), 8½M-46:00 (Hurst), 9M-48:42 (Hurst), 9½M-51:27 (Hurst)
19.03.1898	City and Suburban Grounds, Dublin (grass). 5 miles against Jack Mullen for £100. Mullen won by 45y in 25:50.0. 1M – 4:54 (Hurst), 2M – 10:07 (Mullen), 3M – 15:31 (Mullen), 4M – 20:50 (Hurst).
16.04.1898	Burnden Park, Bolton. 20 miles 1:55:33. Set outright world record for 17 miles and professional world records for 16, 18 and 19 miles. £100. 1M-5:10, 2M-10:30, 3M-15:57, 4M-21:31, 5M-27:13, 6M-32:37, 7M-38:02, 8M-43:25, 9M-48:50, 10M-54:16, 11M-59:48, 1h-11M 60y, 12M-1:05:18, 13M-1:10:56, 14M-1:16:38, 15M-1:22:21, 16M-1:28:14, 17M-1:34:15, 18M-1:40:48, 19M-1:48:05
26.06.1898	Paris-Conflans Marathon. 40 km. 2nd in 2:32:05.
31.07.1898	O'Ryan's Field, High Street, Ponder's End. Oddfellows' Fete and Sports. 1-mile handicap. Off scratch. 2nd (prize, 15s) behind younger brother Ed (150y start)..

01.08.1898	Sittingbourne. Gore Court Park. 4-mile handicap. 1st (scratch) 21:20.0. Run in hot weather.
27.08.1898	Ashton under Lyne. 10 miles against George Crossland for £200. Won. Crossland retired in 7th mile. Hurst was given permission to stop at 7 miles in 37:50.0 (5M-26:50.0).
10.09.1898	Memorial Grounds, Canning Town (cinder, 3 laps to mile). 15 miles against time. Paced by a cyclist, Joe Hurst and Harry Anstead. Strong winds, soft going. 1:23:08.2. 1M – 5:20¾, 2M – 10:42, 3M – 16:00, 4M – 21:25.2, 5M – 26:52, 6M – 32:19.4, 7M – 37:52.2, 8M – 43:25.2, 9M – 49:02.2, 10M – 54:45.2, 11M – 1:00:20, 12M – 1:06:02.8, 13M – 1:11:40.4, 14M – 1:17:36.2.
08.10.1898	Ashton under Lyne. 10 miles against Fred Bacon. Defeated by a yard in 54:43.2. £50 a side. 1M-5:15 (Hurst), 2M-10:26 (Hurst), 3M-16:04 (Bacon), 4M-21:28 (Bacon) 5M-26:48 (Hurst), 6M-32:16 (Hurst), 7M-37:53 (Hurst), 8M-43:20 (Bacon), 9M-49:01 (Hurst), 10M-54:43.0 (Bacon)
29.10.1898	Rochdale. 15 miles against Fred Bacon. Won in 1:23:18. £100. 1M-5:08.6 (Hurst), 2M-10:25.2 (Bacon), 3M-15:41.0 (Bacon), 4M-21:04.2 (Bacon), 5M-26:23.4 (Bacon), 6M-31:52.0 (Hurst), 7M-37:30.8 (Bacon), 7½M-40:11.6 (Bacon), 8M-42:58.8 (Bacon), 9M-48:28.2 (Hurst), 10M-54:59.2 (Hurst), 11M-59:53.0 (Hurst); 12M-1:05:26 (Bacon); 13M-1:11:20 (Hurst), 14M-1:17:36.5 (Hurst)
17.12.1898	Rochdale. 10 miles against Harry Watkins for £100. Defeated. Retired at 6 ¼ miles in approx. 32:50. Splits: 1M 4:52 (40 y to 4:44), 2M 10:14 (150 y to 9:44), 3M 15:32 (200y to 14:52), 4M 20:50 (250y to 20:00), 5M 26:10 (330y to 25:10), 6M 31:30 (350y to 30:20)
01.01.1899	Powderhall, 1-mile handicap. Unplaced (off 40 y). Alex Haddow won.
03.04.1899	Lavender Hill. 1-mile handicap. Off scratch. Unplaced.
23.04.1899	Old Bow Running Grounds,4-mile handicap, retired after 2 miles.
22.05.1899	Sittingbourne, 1-mile handicap. Off 75 yds. Unplaced. 4-mile handicap, 2nd off scratch, £2.
10.06.1899	Lexden Park, Colchester. Hurst v Bacon. 6 miles for £100. Bacon won by 2y in 32:28.0.
26.06.1899	Finney Gardens, Hanley (by Stoke-on-Trent). Ten miles against Fred Bacon for £100. Won by 15 yards. No times reported.
02.07.1899	Paris-Conflans Marathon. 40 km. 2nd in 2:35:12. 1 – A. Charbonnel 2:33:10.
31.07.1899	Catford grounds. 20 miles against time. Retired after covering 13 miles 2 ½ laps in 1:20:05. Splits: 1M-5:16.5, 2M-10:41.3, 3M-16:11.3, 4M-21:41.5, 5M-27:17.0, 6M-32:57.3, 7M-38:36, 8M-44:20.5, 9M-50:02, 10M-56:25, 11M-1:03:15, 12M-1:09:21, 13M-1:15:20.

07.08.1899	Gore Court Park, Sittingbourne. 10-mile scratch race for £29. 6 laps to the mile. Harry Watkins won in 52:05.0. Hurst finished 2nd approx. 370y behind Watkins in ca. 53:20. Splits: 5M-26:16, 6M-31:25, 7M-36:35, 8M-42:37, 9M-47:48 (estimates)
03.09.1899	Old Bow Running Grounds, 10-mile handicap, 1 ½ laps start (virtual scratch), non-starter.
11.09.1899	Oddfellows' Fete. Chase Side House Grounds. Enfield. Unplaced off scratch in 1-mile handicap. 18 started. Narrow track and sharp bends.
11.11.1899	Ashton under Lyne. 5 miles against Mick O'Neill for £100. O'Neill won by 50 yds. in 26:45.8. Hurst stopped 50 yds. from tape and walked in. Windy. 1M – 5:21, 2M – 10:45, 3M – 16:08.6, 4M – 21:34.6
13.04.1900	Nunhead. Brown's Ground. 4-mile handicap. 1st off 30 y. No time taken.
16.04.1900	Aylesford Athletic Ground, 4-mile handicap. 4th off scratch.
27.06.1900	Southport Sports Grounds. 10 miles against Mick O'Neill. O'Neill won by 20y in 54:33. Hurst 54:37. £100. 1M – 5:12, 2M – 10:30, 3M – 15:50, 4M – 21:13½, 5M – 26:36, 6M – 31:50, 7M – 37:24, 8M – 42:49, 9M – 48:24, 10M – 54:37.
30.06.1900	Southampton Football Ground. 10 miles against Fred Bacon. Defeated by 1 ½ yds. Bacon 54:10.0. Hurst 54:10.3. 1M – 5:08, 2M – 10:15, 3M – 15:26, 4M – 21:00, 5M – 26:05, 6M – 31:24, 7M – 37:00, 8M – 42:23, 9M – 48:02.
08.07.1900	Conflans-Paris Marathon. 40 km. 1st in 2:26:47.4. 1000F.
05.08.1900	Paris (Vincennes). Six Hour World Championship for Professionals (incorporated into 1900 Olympic Games). Retd. after covering 61km in 5h 15min. 1st Victor Bagré 72.545 km (world record). Splits: 10 km 38:46.0; 1h – 15.59 km; 20 km – 1:20:05.2; 2h – 29.2 km; 30 km – 2:03; 35 km – 2:25:31.4 (world record); 40 km – 2:48:05; 3h – 42,503m; 45 km – 3:13:29; 50 km – 3:36:45 (world record); 4h – 54,136m (world record).
23.08.1900	Vincennes. 20 miles for 750F against Charbonnel. Cancelled.
10.09.1900	Oddfellows' Fete. Chase Side House Grounds. Enfield. Retd. in mile hcp off 60y.
06.10.1900	Wood Green, London. 20 miles. 1:53:42¼ (world professional record). See table for splits.
17.11.1900	Tee-To-Tum Grounds, Stamford Hill. 50 miles against Billy Saward for £25 a-side. Saward withdrew and forfeited his deposit.
03.02.1901	Old Bow Running Grounds. 4-mile handicap. 4th off 100y.
18.03.1901	White Hart Grounds, Tottenham Hale. 4-mile handicap. 1st off scratch in 21:50.0.

05.04.1901	Nunhead. Brown's Ground. 4-mile handicap. 1 – Ted Shepherd (80 yds start), 2 – Abe Crudgington (165); 3 – Len Hurst (15 y). Shepherd won by 100 yds, 2 yds between 2nd and 3rd. No times reported.
08.04.1901	Lavender Hill. 1st in 440y handicap off 47y. 2nd to H. Jones (Enfield, 40y) in mile hcp off 60y. Defeated H. Jones over 2 miles for £5.
06.05.1901	Old Bow Running Grounds. 4-mile handicap. 4th off 120 yds. No times reported.
27.05.1901	Sittingbourne. Gore Court Park. 4-mile handicap. 3rd. 1, 22:05.0 Tom Still (Upchurch, 250 yds start); 2, 22:07e (10 yds) Arthur Flaunty (London, 420 yds start); 3, Len Hurst (London, 30 yds start) (50 yds) 22:15e; 4, Joe Hurst (London, 420 yds start).
07.07.1901	Paris-Conflans Marathon. 40 km. 1st in 2:34:52.4.
17.08.1901	Grays, Essex. Twenty Miles Professional Championship. £50. Defeated Ted Shepherd (Higham). Allowed to stop after covering 13 ¼ miles in 1:16:36¾. 700 spectators. 1M – 5:43.5 (Shepherd), 2M-11:50 (Hurst); 3M-17:50 (Shepherd), 4M-23:13 (Hurst), 5M-28:39, 6M-34:17½, 7M-40:09¼, 9M-51:48½, 10M-57:44½ (Shepherd 58:50½), 11M-1:03:51¾, 12M-1:09:45, 13M-1:15:12¾
31.08.1901	Eureka Athletic Ground, Lincoln Road, Ponders End. 20-mile race against time. Track 5 laps to mile. Len and Joe Hurst, running simultaneously, jointly covered 20 miles in 57:15 for a purse of gold "subscribed by some local sporting gentlemen". 10M 930y (= 54:51 for 10M). Inclement weather.
23.09.1901	Tee-To-Tum Grounds, Stamford Hill. Twenty-five Mile Championship. Hurst awarded race after Bob Hallen, USA, retired. Forced to stop by crowd invasion at 13 miles less 30y in 1:17:45 (5M – 30:23¼, 12M – 1:11:58.5).
05.10.1901	Stamford Hill, Tee-To-Tum Grounds. 10 miles against time. 1M-5:21 ¼, 2M – 10:49.5, 3M – 16:16 ¾, 4M – 21:51.5, 5M – 27:27½, 6M – 33:09.0, 7M – 38:53 ¼, 8M – 44:41.5; 9M – 50:29 ¼, 10M - 56:09.5. An attempt on the 15 miles record had originally been planned but the distance was reduced to 10 miles owing to the wet and windy conditions.
26.10.1901	Tee-To-Tum Grounds, Stamford Hill. 4-mile handicap. Scratch. Hurst ran 3 miles and retired.
16.11.1901	Tee-To-Tum Grounds, Stamford Hill. 25 miles against time for £50. Retired after completing 14 ¾ miles in 1:29:27 ¾ 1M-5:55.5, 2M-11:49 ¼, 3M-17:40 ¾, 4M-23:35, 5M-29:30.5, 6M-35:29.5, 7M-41:25 ¼, 8M-47:26 ¼; 9M-53:28 ¾, 10M-59:36.5, 1h – 10M 105y, 11M-1:05:48.5, 12M-1:11:58 ¾; 13M-1:18:12.5, 14M-1:24:29.5.

10.02.1902	Madison Square Garden, NYC. Six day 12 hours per day team race. The Hurst Bros. retired at 4 a.m. on day 6 after covering 494.3 miles in 120 hours.
28.03.1902	Stamford Hill. Tee-to-Tum Grounds. 10 Mile Professional Championship of the World. 1 – Fred Bacon 56:10.6 £10; 2 – Len Hurst 57:00e [300 yds, sprinted home] £2; 3 – Tom Collins 58:20e [350 yds] £1 10s; 4 – Ted Shepherd; 5 - Abe Crudgington
03.05.1902	Alloa Recreation Ground. 10 miles against Fred Bacon. Defeated by 12 yds, 54:24.0 to 54:26.5. £50. 4M-21:49.
19.05.1902	Sittingbourne. Gore Court Park. 4-mile handicap. 4th off 200y. 230y behind winner. Tom Still (Upchurch) won in 20:56.0 off 300y.
20.05.1902	Rainham. Recreation Grounds. 4-mile handicap. Unplaced (scratch). P. Pearson (Cliffe) won in 20:46.0 off 70y.
02.06.1902	Nunhead. Brown's Ground. 4-mile handicap. 6th off 70y. 1 – Tom Olliver (Brighton) 55y
26.06.1902	Stamford Hill. Tee-to-Tum Grounds. (5 laps to the mile). 15 miles against Fred Bacon for £25 a side and half net gate receipts. Won. Hurst was given permission to stop after covering 8.2 miles in 47:34. 1M-5:28, 2M-11:10, 3M-16:52, 4M-22:45, 5M-28:29, 6M-35:23, 7M-41:11, 8M-46:32
06.07.1902	Achères-Paris Marathon. 40 km. 3rd in 2:56:40. 1 – Albert Charbonnel 2:52:05.
13.07.1902	Buffalo Velodrome, Neuilly, Paris. 10,000m European Championship. 3rd. 1 – Fred Bacon 34:26.6 £5, 2 – Gustave Thomas 34:28.5e (10m) £3; 3 – Len Hurst (100m behind winner) £2 34:47.5e; 4 – Albert Charbonnel (350m) £1
14.07.1902	Buffalo Velodrome, Paris. 1,500m European Championship. 2nd in 4:31.5e. Gustave Thomas won by 8m in 4:30.0.
20.07.1902	Buffalo Velodrome, Paris. 1-hour race. ENG v FRA. 1st 16,870m (10 miles 858 yards); 2 – Albert Charbonnel 16,865m; 3 – Fred Bacon 16,665m; 4 – Gustave Thomas (retd.). The English runners won the team contest, each receiving the equivalent of £16. 5 km – 16:49.0, 10 km – 34:43.8, 15 km – 53:34.4.
27.07.1902	Buffalo Velodrome, Paris. 1-hour race. 1st. 16,700m; 2 – Fred Bacon 16,650m; 3 – Albert Charbonnel 16,200m; 4 – Gustave Thomas retd. Windy conditions. 5 km – 17:11.4, 10 km – 35:08.4, 15 km – 53:52.2.
13.09.1902	Bridge Road Recreation Ground, Grays, Essex. 6-mile open handicap for prizes worth £10 10s. 110y start. 2nd (just failed to win). £2. No times reported. Starters also included: William Swan (240y), Tom Jackson (380y), Gustave Thomas (30y), Abe Crudgington (200y), Ted Shepherd (170y), Tom Still (200y), Wm. Saward (340y)

26.12.1902	Old Bow Grounds. 6½ laps to the mile. 10-mile handicap for a G. & S. silver champion's belt. 15 starters. Hurst (scratch) won by 20 yards. No times reported.
04.01.1903	Old Bow Grounds. 10 miles against Tom Jackson (4 laps start) for £5. Hurst was impeded by spectators 130 yards from the finish. Tom Connor, the proprietor, declared the match a 'no race' and donated the prize money to a local hospital. Jackson was first past the post in 57:52 but on the last lap Hurst had been leading by 50 yards. Hurst's splits: 2M-10:40, 4M-21:50, 5M-27:30, 8M-45:40.
23.03.1903	Stamford Hill. Tee-to-Tum Grounds. 15 hours against Charlie Hart for £100. Won with 89.6 miles (143.78 km). 1h – 9.6M; 2h – 18.4M; 3h – 26.0M; 4h – 31.8M; 5h – 38.2M; 6h – 44.2M; 50M-6:53:15; 7h – 50.7M; 8h – 56.2M; 9h – 60.0M; 10h – 63.8M (102.7 km); 11h – 68.0M; 12h - 73.8M; 13h – 78.4M; 14h – 83.8M
10.04.1903	Stamford Hill. Tee-to-Tum Grounds. 10 Miles Professional Championship of the World (30 entries). 4th. 1 – Gustave Thomas (France) 54:34.0; 2 – Fred Bacon, 60y [54:46]; 3 – Tom E. Olliver, 60y [54:58]; 4 – Len Hurst, 350y [56:20] [Hurst's splits: 1M – 5:10, 2M – 10:30, 3M – 15:55, 4M – 21:06, 8M –44:20]
13.04.1903	Vicarage Field, Barking. 10-mile handicap. 1, 57:25.0 Gustave Thomas (150 yds start); 2, 57:31e [30 yds.] Hurst (200 yds. start); 3, 58:30e Tom Jackson (390 yds start). Rough grass track, six laps to mile.
14.04.1903	Dagenham, Bull Hotel grounds. 4-mile handicap. Started as back-marker off 200 yards. Unplaced.
25.05.1903	Memorial Ground, Canning Town. Also-ran in mile handicap off 90y. Also-ran in 4-mile handicap off 70y.
01.06.1903	Stamford Hill. Tee-to-Tum Grounds. 6th in mile handicap off 70y.
01.06.1903	Vicarage Field, Barking. 5 miles against Tom Collins. 1st. Collins retired 2 laps from the finish.
02.06.1903	Stamford Hill. Tee-to-Tum Grounds. 4-mile handicap. Retd. after running only two laps.
08.06.1903	Ponder's End. Match against time for a wager. 10 miles from Brewer's Hotel to Cheshunt & back on the main London to Hertford Road. Hurst completed the distance in 56 mins. and won the wager (to beat the hour).
20.06.1903	London to Brighton race, 52 ¼ miles. Won in a record time of 6:34:50.
18.07.1903	Memorial Grounds, Canning Town. 5-mile hcp. Retd. after 2 miles due to illness.
01.08.1903	Vicarage Field, Barking. 4-mile level race. 2nd in approx. 23:25 (George Matthews, Bow, won by 5y in 23:24).

27.08.1903	Preston Park, Brighton, 25 miles. 2:33:42. World record. 1M-6:06, 2M-12:07, 3M-18:00, 4M-23:49, 5M-29:43, 6M-35:37, 7M-41:33, 8M-47:32, 9M-53_35, 10M-59:37, 1M-1:05:40, 12M-1:11:42, 13M-17:46, 14M-1:23:49, 15M-1:29:53, 16M-1:36:02, 17M-1:42:20, 18M-1:48:35, 19M-1:54:56, 20M-2:01:12, 22M-2:07:37, 22M-2:14:05, 23M-2:20:40, 24M-2:27:22
29.08.1903	Eley's Athletic Ground, Ponder's End. 4 miles against 'A. Aldridge' (aka George Matthews) for a purse of gold. Won by 1 yard.
26.09.1903	Ponder's End. Eley's Athletic Ground. 6 miles. Easily defeated Fred Morris and W. Kemp, who ran 3 miles each.
15.11.1903	Paris (Buffalo Stadium), 50 miles. Retired after 5 hours. 1 – Gustave Thomas 6:13:29.2; 2 – Edouard Cibot 6:23:28; 3 – Albert Charbonnel 6:31:14 Splits: 1h – 15.0 km (3), 2h - 29.45 km (2), 3h - 42.0 km (3), 4h - 52.5 km (3), 5h - 56.5 km (5).
03.01.1904	Homerton. Angel road Athletic Grounds. 4 miles against Oliver Steele (250 yds start). Defeated.
01.08.1904	Barking Bank Holiday Sports. 4 miles against Tom Collins. Retd. soon after start due to foot injury.
15.09.1907	Rouen-Paris road race. 156 km. Retired after only 5km due to knee trouble.
28.12.1907	Rochdale. 30 miles against Andrew Johnson for £50 a-side. Def. Retd. in 20th mile when 1¾ miles behind Johnson. [1M-6:06, 10M-1:04, 13M-1:25, 15M-1:39:35, 18½M-2:05, 19½M-2:14]
10.10.1908	Evening News Marathon, London, 26M 585y. 25th in 3:23:00.6.

ACKNOWLEDGEMENTS

It would be foolish to claim that this biography is exhaustive given that it portrays a long-dead Victorian-era professional runner whose only written legacy is a one-page flyer and a brief item in another runner's autobiography. Without Andy Milroy's invaluable groundwork in the pre-internet days, it wouldn't have been possible to give anywhere near as rounded a picture of Len Hurst, the man and the athlete, as is hopefully the case. His prescient interview with the late Alf Hurst was the foundation upon which this story is built. Online resources, that have only become available in recent years, have made it possible to identify and delineate the most important milestones in the life of our main protagonist.

Even a decade ago, this would have been an impossible task. As with any undertaking, a little luck helps. Was it fate or was it fortune that brought Len Hurst to Paris for the marathon race in 1896? This was the turning point not only for his career but also for this story. When Len first visited the French capital, sports photography was still in its infancy. But Paris was a forward-looking city and their denizens were quick to embrace all things novel. Parisian illustrated magazines from the dawn of sports photography have provided this biography with an added visual dimension that is unusual for the period. In the 15 years since the start of this project, more and more small pieces of the puzzle have come to light. Even if many pieces of the puzzle are still missing, and we must assume so, there comes a time to draw the line and to unleash the story. This, of course, carries the risk of valuable new material emerging immediately afterwards, which I am sure will happen. Unfortunately, all writers have an expiration date and have to make compromises. In the hope that no one has been overlooked, my special thanks go to the following individuals and organisations (who are listed below in no particular order):

Andy Milroy, Alfred Hurst, Ian Champion, Peter Lovesey, Ron Skelcher, Road Runners Club, Sittingbourne Museum, Sittingbourne Library, Martin Pile, Kevin Kelly.

I would also like to thank Peter Lovesey for his book title suggestions, one of which I liked a lot.

Alex Wilson - 25 July 2019

BIBLIOGRAPHY AND SOURCES

A. BOOKS

Hubert Hamacher, Leichtathetik im 19. Jahrhundert Band 1, DGLD, Germany, 2003

Karl Lennartz, Marathonlauf – Von den Anfängen bis van Aaken, DGLD, Erkrath, 2005

A. R. Downer, Running Recollections and How To Train, Gale & Polden, London, 1900

Charles Harper, The Brighton Road, Cecil Palmer, London, 1922

Dave Roberts, Distance Running Records, R.R.C., 1961

Warren Roe, Front Runners, The Book Guild Ltd, Lewes, 2002

Richard O. Watson, 'Choppy' Warburton, E Wileybooks, Eastbourne, 2006

Arthur F. H. Newton, Running in three continents, H. F. & G. Witherby, London, 1940

Arthur F. H. Newton, Running, H. F. & G. Witherby, London, 1935

Rob Hadgraft, Tea With Mr Newton, Desert Island Books, 2010

Sporting Chronicle Annual for 1911, Sporting Chronicle, Manchester, 1912

B. WEBSITES

https://www.britishnewspaperarchive.co.uk/
https://pubwiki.co.uk/ (formerly www.pubshistory.com)
https://www.ancestry.co.uk
https://www.bl.uk/
http://galica.fr
http://anno.onb.ac.at/
https://www.roadrunnersclub.org.uk/

https://arrs.run
http://mapco.net/london.htm
https://www.wikipedia.org/

C. MAGAZINES AND NEWSPAPERS

Allgemeine Sport-Zeitung

Alloa Advertiser

Athletic Review

Athletics Weekly

Barking, East Ham & Ilford Advertiser

Bells Life in London

Brighton Gazette

Brighton Argus

Brooklyn Daily Eagle

Chelmsford Chronicle

Daily Mirror

East Kent Gazette

[London] Echo

Edinburgh Evening News

Essex Standard

[London] Evening News

[Cardiff] Evening Express

Evening Telegram (New York)

Freeman's Journal (Dublin)

Hampshire Advertiser

Hastings and St. Leonard's Observer

Illustrated Police News

Kentish Advertiser

La Vie au grand air (Paris)

L'Actualité (Paris)

L'Auto-Vélo (Paris)

L'Écho de Paris (Paris)

L'Illustration (Paris)

Le Matin (Paris)

Le Petit Journal (Paris)

Le Petit Parisien (Paris)

Le Sport universel illustré (Paris)

Lloyd's Weekly Newspaper

London Daily News

Manchester Evening News

Manchester Guardian

Middlesex Gazette

Morning Post

News of the World

Nottingham Evening Post

North Middlesex Standard

Otago Witness

Pall Mall Gazette

Pearson's Athletic Record

Road Runners Club Newsletter

Sheffield Daily Telegraph

South London Harriers Gazette

Suffolk and Essex Free Press

The Sketch

The Sportsman

The Sporting Life

The World (New York)

Weekly Guardian

ND - #0106 - 270225 - C0 - 234/156/10 - PB - 9781780915708 - Gloss Lamination